JOAN LUNDEN'S
HEALTHY COOKING

ALSO BY JOAN LUNDEN

Good Morning, I'm Joan Lunden
with Ardy Friedberg

JOAN LUNDEN'S HEALTHY COOKING

Joan Lunden
AND *Laura Morton*

WITH PHOTOGRAPHS BY *Tom Eckerle*
RECIPE TESTER: *Sara Moulton*

LITTLE, BROWN AND COMPANY
Boston   New York   Toronto   London

First Edition

"Red Hot Salsa" from *Biker Billy Cooks with Fire* by Bill Hufnagle. Text Copyright © 1995 by Bill Hufnagle. By permission of William Morrow and Company, Inc.
"Apple Pie Crust," "Chili Burgers," and "Jewel of the Nile Kebabs" from *The Eating Well Rush Hour Cookbook* by the editors of *Eating Well,* Patsy Jamieson, Test Kitchen Director. Copyright © 1994 by Eating Well Books. By permission of *Eating Well Magazine.*
"When I'm Back on My Feet Again" by Diane Warren © 1989, 1990 REALSONGS All rights reserved. By permission of Warner Chappell Music, Inc.

Library of Congress Cataloging-in-Publication Data

Lunden, Joan.
    Healthy cooking with Joan Lunden / Joan Lunden and Laura Morton ;
with photographs by Tom Eckerle.
       p.   cm.
    Includes index.
    ISBN 0-316-53588-5 (hc)
    1. Cookery.   2. Low-fat diet — Recipes.   3. Lunden, Joan.
    I. Morton, Laura.   II. Title.
TX714.L86   1996
641.5'63 — dc20   95-43355

10 9 8 7 6 5 4

Published simultaneously in Canada by Little, Brown & Company (Canada) Limited

Printed in the United States of America

To all of the words that have touched me and that have changed my life. These are just a few . . .

❖

You can be anything you want to be; the word "impossible" isn't in our dictionary.

— *Gladyce Blunden* (Joan's mom)

Search for the hero inside yourself,
Until you find the key to your life.

— *From the musical group M People song,*
Search for the Hero (*Bizarre Fruit* compact disc)

You can't stop the waves, but you can learn to surf.

— *Jon Kabat-Zinn*
Wherever You Go, There You Are (*Mindfulness Meditation in Everyday Life*)

Gonna break these chains around me
Gonna learn to fly again.
May be hard, but I'll do it
When I'm back on my feet again.

— *Michael Bolton* (*Soul Provider* compact disc)

Health is not just the absence of a disease. It's an inner joyfulness that should be ours all the time — a state of positive well-being.

— *Deepak Chopra, M.D.,* Journey Into Healing

The future belongs to those who can smell it coming.

— *RuPaul* (SuperModel of the World *compact disc*)

CONTENTS

A C K N O W L E D G M E N T S

There are a lot of people who worked on this project I want to thank. But before I do, I thought that I would explain to you how I came to write a cookbook. After losing so much weight in front of millions of Americans, people were constantly asking me to share with them the program that helped me lose and keep off my weight. So it was a natural next step to do my own exercise video. I turned to someone who had produced some of the most successful videos on the market, Laura Morton.

In August of 1994, shortly after we had finished shooting *Workout America,* I took a vacation in the New York resort community known as the Hamptons. I was there to compete in the Hampton Classic Horse Show. Laura happened to be there that same week. After a dinner party at my home one night, the discussion turned to new projects. She felt that it was a logical progression to write a cookbook to accompany the exercise video. After all, I had totally reconditioned my eating habits as part of my weight loss. Being a fellow Virgo, somehow I just knew that Laura's half-baked idea would make it to the table. Out of the strangest circumstances come the most unexpected opportunities.

Sure enough, seven months later, I found myself meeting publisher after publisher, describing to them what you now see in the following pages. Our book agent, Al Lowman of Authors and Artists Group, cleverly crafted a publishing deal for us with Little, Brown. Through his expertise and love of this project, he helped Laura and me choose the perfect home for our book. We knew Little, Brown was the right choice for this project by the tremendous support our editor, Jennifer Josephy, offered. Her openness to our ideas allowed us to be our creative selves. Our sincere thanks to Jennifer, Bill Phillips, and everyone at Little, Brown.

Suddenly, though, I was faced with the task of creating a cookbook. I knew that if we were to meet our self-imposed deadline for delivery, it would take a small army of people to get it done. When in doubt, turn to your friends, as I always say. Who better to support such an undertaking?

I called our good friend Elise Silvestri, who found herself at the early stages of pregnancy at the time and needed to leave her high-pressure job producing the *Sally Jesse Raphael* show. Timing is everything in life. Elise agreed to help us, and she did an unbelievable job interviewing all our experts for the book. She left no stone unturned. I am certain that we could not have pulled this off without her enthusiasm and professionalism. (And to her husband, Michael, thanks from the bottom of our hearts for understanding those long work sessions.) Incidentally, Elise claims that because of the low-fat recipes we tasted day in and day out, she gained only half the amount of weight from this pregnancy as she did with her first.

We also turned to another close friend, Scot Evans, who came through for us in so many ways and so many times. Scot helped us with our daily production needs, but more important, he provided us with unconditional moral support.

After pulling the core group together, it was time to get the rest of the team in order. Sara Moulton, who for years has prepared all the dishes you see made on *GMA,* became indispensable to this project, agreeing to become our food tester and recipe writer. We knew that she had a lot on her plate, so to speak, but she still managed to meet our every demand, and always with a smile. We are forever grateful to you, Sara, and your entire team at *Gourmet* magazine, including Suzanne Yearly and Heather Hughs. Barb Durbin did all our nutritional analyses, and her wit and humor made this rather stale task as much fun as it could be. Thanks, Barb. You should take your act on the road.

You can't write a cookbook without testing the recipes on real people, and that's where Bonnie Conklin, my children's nanny for ten years, entered the picture. Between Bonnie and us, we cooked and fussed and tried, and tried again until we got them right. This was no easy task, for the critics were none other than my own children. Thank you to my girls, who patiently tried every dish, even if they didn't like it. You're the lights of my life.

They say that every picture tells a story, so turnabout is fair play. Some of my pet peeves about cookbooks are (1) if they have no pictures, (2) if the recipes opposite the pictures don't match, and (3) pictures where you're not sure if you're supposed to be looking at the wine glasses or the food. We turned to Tom Eckerle and his brilliance to visually translate our ideas and recipes. Believe me, he is the Scavullo of food. With the help of Roscoe Betsill, our food stylist, and his assistant, Michael Pederson, the food looks so alive that it practically jumps off the page. Ceci Gallini did an amazing job of creating the look of the photos through her meticulous prop styling.

And no photo shoot would be complete without hair styling and makeup, so Mark Daniel Fonzi, who always styles my hair for *GMA,* and Michelle Cutler, my makeup artist for *GMA,* once again, thanks for doing what you do. And thanks to Antonio Dileo, who also styled hair for our location shoots for this book. You are all the best.

Our food photos are only part of the photos included in this book. It took another small army of people to help pull this to-

Laura Morton, Joan, and Elise Silvestri

gether for us. Samantha Berg, my former personal assistant, worked very closely with Ida Astute at the ABC photo archives to look back and research photos taken of me over the years. Without their diligence and help, we would have just had an ordinary cookbook. I know I love seeing behind-the-scene photos, and you may even recognize a face or two. Jill Alpert, my current assistant, and my good friend Debbie Bergenfeld also worked endlessly to help make this book possible. Debbie's knowledge, having been my assistant from 1984 to 1992, was invaluable. And speaking of invaluable, Anne-Marie Riccitelli, who handles my publicity at ABC, has always had ingenious foresight and understanding when it comes to the proper handling of my projects. Thank you all for your perseverance. It was an essential ingredient in making this book possible.

To all of the contributing chefs, authors, and experts, thank you for allowing us to tap into your greatness. Together, I think we offer a very special book to the reader. A special thank you to Barbara Brandt, my personal trainer and my very good friend, without whom my physical transformation would not have been possible. You changed my life forever.

Well, that's the way it happened. To be able to work with the people you love the most in life, and to have fun in the process, is one of the greatest experiences people can give themselves. When it stops being fun, I don't want to do it anymore, and this never stopped being fun.

We always like to save the best for dessert. So the icing on this cake is our families. Jamie, Lindsay, and Sarah . . . my heart is filled by you. And to my mom, Gladyce: I may not have attempted this challenge had you not instilled in me at an early age that nothing is impossible. And for Laura: Eunice and Milt, you should know that you are her greatest inspiration. Finally, to our guardian angels . . . to my dad, Erle, and to Laura's mom, Suzanne, we know that you're looking down on us with a smile.

PART ONE

INTRODUCTION

Because my work brings me into so many homes every weekday morning, a lot of people look upon me as a friend. I get thousands of letters from viewers. I talk with them after speeches, in airports — you name it. And the three things most people want to know about me these days are:

• What time do you get up?
• What time do you go to bed?
• *How* did you lose all of that weight?

The answers are:

• 4:00 A.M.
• 9:00 P.M.
• Read this book.

Before I lost more than fifty pounds, I used to be asked one more question: "When are you expecting?"

The memory of that question still stings, because I heard it all too often when I was not pregnant at all. I always tried to be polite in my response, which was usually that I'd just had a baby. Of course, I knew that my "baby" was really pushing two years old.

❖

This is the story of my journey to fitness. I call it a journey because this was not a decision I just woke up one morning and made.

It took a lot of attempts and failures before I figured out a way to succeed. It took years of emotional and physical ups and downs.

I grew up in the fifties and sixties, when America was a meat-and-potatoes nation. We were a country consumed with causes and world issues, not overly concerned with our health and well-being. I lived on french fries, hamburgers, chocolate shakes, pizza, pasta, all that stuff. I would never have *thought* of eating a piece of broiled fish or sushi — yuck!

My mom was, and still is, a good cook. She always had something on the stove or in the oven. When I came home from school, the house would be filled with the aroma of onions frying in butter or a potato casserole baking. Mom put cream sauce on everything — but so did everyone's mom. In those days, if your sauce wasn't thick enough, you added a can of cream of mushroom soup. Batter not rich enough? Just add more butter. That was our way of life pre-NC (pre–nouvelle cuisine). There was certainly no consideration given to the possible future effects of this high-fat diet. I took a lot of that comfort-food consciousness with me when I left Sacramento, and over the years, I've had to find a way to satisfy my desire for my mom's delicious meals, without all the unwanted fat and calories.

❖

In collecting my thoughts for this book, I literally mapped out the progression of my weight gain. (I've included my timeline at the end of this introduction.) It's clear to see that in times of stress, anger, and unhappiness, my weight went up.

For all those years, food was my friend and my enemy. When I woke up in the morning, one of the first things I thought about was how I was going to deal with food. How would I stick to my diet-of-the-week? How would I deal with feeling deprived, famished, and exhausted from what little I was "allowed" to eat? In the evening, I'd comfort and reward myself with food.

The extra pounds I was carrying were weighing my life down. Was it food that was making me miserable, or was it that I was miserable and turning to food? This was the vicious cycle I had to break.

And I tried. I went on every diet there was to go on. Atkins, Scarsdale, grapefruit, high protein, the one that makes your breath smell bad — I mean, I would eat only one food for months! I did every stupid, idiotic diet that there ever was. And I'd have a little bit of success.

But a diet is a false state of living that you can't maintain. At some point I'd go off it, and I'd gain again. And then I'd say, "Screw it. I'm just back where I was. I've failed." Then time would pass, I'd find another diet, and the cycle of frustration started once again.

❖

I was approaching my thirty-ninth birthday, and hosting two national daily talk shows: *Good Morning America* and *Every Day*. I was trying to balance my career with three beautiful children and a home life. I also knew that I was facing the inevitable demise of my marriage, which meant the added pressure of being "out there" again as a single woman. The time had come to change once and for all. The reasons to lose the weight and keep it off far outnumbered my excuses.

I tackled this seemingly impossible task much the same way I approach my work at *Good Morning America*. I sought out the experts. In my job, I have the rare opportunity to interview the best on a daily basis. I have picked the brains of the world's foremost nutritionists. I've hit the mat with the top fitness experts. I've even stirred the pot with just about every great chef in the country. With their help and advice, I have shed fifty pounds, dramatically cut my medical risks, and now find myself enjoying a high-spirited lifestyle filled with challenging (and fun!) physical activity.

Five years ago, I had trouble doing a few sit-ups. I never would have dreamed of a vacation where I'd bicycle through France, climb the mountains of Alaska, or scuba dive the coral reefs of the Caribbean. Much more important, when one of my daughters says, "Mommy, let's go bike riding!" now I can say yes and truly want to share that experience.

My new fit life has opened up a world of possibilities. This story has a happy ending, because I found fitness at forty. It's never too late!

Let's face it, you can't diet forever. There will always be an excuse for not losing the weight or not eating a healthy meal. How many calories do you think you've counted during your lifetime? Millions? I've come to realize that counting calories is not what it should be about. I've overheard my sixteen-year-old daughter's friends talk about how much fat is in this and how many calories are in that! I don't think I knew anything, let alone cared, about fat and calories at sixteen. I've made these changes not only to benefit myself but to be able to teach my daughters good eating habits, so they don't become "diet-addicted" adults.

Now I think "diet" is a bad word. This book is not about dieting. It's really about taking the next step beyond dieting. I never knew how to make healthy choices. I never knew there were delicious alternatives to the bland routine of "shoulds" like carrot sticks, water-packed tuna, and turkey breast.

But there's no magic bullet. It takes time, effort, desire, and arming yourself with tactics and education. It's about learning to use those elements that we know work, like fat reduction and portion control, and applying those to everyday cooking. It's about identifying your vulnerable points, your habits, what it is you're doing wrong, and then breaking those habits and replacing them with things you can do right — things that you enjoy!

During my five-year journey to fitness, I have collected and perfected hundreds of easy recipes that meet my newfound nutritional standards — and just as important, taste delicious. I'm not only antidiet, I'm antideprivation. Living a life of deprivation isn't fun, and I want to enjoy life.

❖

My decision to write this book was motivated by two things. First, I found that the more I changed, the better I felt about myself. The better I was feeling, the more I wanted to continue changing. I felt like an explorer on a treasure hunt, only to discover that the treasure had been buried inside of me the whole time.

Often, when people go through big changes in their lives, they get this unbounded enthusiasm to share them with others — and I definitely got bitten by that bug! If you can honestly sense and feel how wonderful it is to be on the other end of that timeline, maybe you'll say, "I want what she ordered. I want what *she's* having, thank you!" Maybe you'll go there with me. And that would be incredibly great.

Or maybe you'll just go part of the way and make a few changes, or you'll just feel less alone. During my journey, I have come to learn that my struggle with food and weight loss is a common one. But most of us struggle with this battle of the bulge in isolation. I know I did.

My second reason is selfish. Sharing my success and making myself a positive role model are great motivations for me to stay this way! It reminds me of an interview I did with Betty Ford for one of my ABC-TV "Behind Closed Doors" specials. She told me the reason she opened the Betty Ford Treatment Center and is often a speaker there is to reinforce her own sobriety as a recovering alcoholic. That philosophy really hit home with me, and I think it's been pivotal in keeping the weight off.

I guess the most ironic part of writing this book is that so many people, to this day, can't remember me ever being overweight. I've had a lot of sleepless nights and endless debates with friends and family over just how much I should reveal. I am putting my absolute heart and soul on the line here. I mean, who would ever *want* to remind people that they used to be overweight — especially someone in the public eye? It's something that you've hidden all your life, and all of a sudden you're going to talk about it?

This is from my guts. This is talking about my failures. I struggled with food in isolation, and I was ashamed of it. I spent years hiding the problem, becoming an expert at camouflage dressing and trying to keep those "heavy" pictures out of the papers. Now here I am, exposing all of those things I used to cover up.

❖

I am what you might call a "cookbook junkie." I can never leave a bookstore without the latest and greatest easy-to-use/good-for-you/healthy-eating/low-fat/low-calorie/vegetarian/you-name-it cookbook. Let's face it, there's no real shortage of selection out there on these topics.

So why am I writing a cookbook? Because, like men, I can't live with them and can't live without them. So I've taken all the elements I like about these books and blended them into one terrific, easy-to-use, nonfrustrating package. (If only it were that easy with men!)

Inside these pages you will find a selection of my favorite healthy and delicious recipes. I've kept them simple, to go with an active lifestyle. Following this kind of "liveable" cooking plan and a regular exercise program will help you lose the weight — and keep the weight off. I know it can, because it has really worked for me.

I have *hundreds* of cookbooks in my home. But there are always a half-dozen or so that have the sticky pages, because those are the ones I use. I hope this will become one of your sticky-page books. That would make me really happy.

TIMELINE

❖ *New baby*
❖ *Full-time job*
❖ *Lose 50 pounds gained by pregnancy*
❖ *Weigh 140*

❖ *Start hosting GMA*
❖ *Pregnant with first child*
❖ *Weigh 130*

❖ *Workload at a new high with two toddlers at home*
❖ *No real vacation in over two years*
❖ *Marriage troubles*
❖ *Lose only 40 of the 60 pounds gained*

27	29	30	31	33	34	37

❖ *Newlywed*
❖ *Footloose and fancy-free*
❖ *At 5'7½", 125 pounds*

❖ *Gain 60 pounds from pregnancy*
❖ *Weigh 190*

❖ *Pregnant with second child*
❖ *Increased workload with two national daily talk shows*
❖ *Gain 60 pounds from pregnancy*

❖ *Third pregnancy*
❖ *Pressure to keep marriage together*
❖ *Pressure to keep up intense workload*
❖ *Gain 40 pounds from pregnancy*
❖ *Carrying a 10½-pound baby*

* Three children at home
* Workload impossible
* No time to exercise
* Lose 20 pounds gained by pregnancy
* Although I try, panic sets in as I cannot lose more weight

CRAIG BLANKENHORN

* Tired of my own excuses
* Need a big turn-around
* Don't feel femi-nine or sexy
* Hide to undress
* On a good day, I am wearing size 14
* Give myself one year to get a grip on life

* Stop dieting; now learning every day how to make

ROBERT MILAZZO/ABC

better, healthier choices for me and my family, for a healthier lifestyle
* Stress is still high, workload is immense, getting divorced, but not using food for comfort
* Relieving stress through exercise

| 38 | 38½ | 39 | 40 | 41 | 45 |

---

* Unhappy marriage
* Using food for comfort
* Can't use "just had a baby" excuse anymore
* I should know better
* Try every fad diet
* How did I get here?
* Weigh 180

LARRY BUSACA

* After one year of a closely supervised weight loss and fitness program, I have educated myself on healthy eating and have lost 50 pounds
* Now wearing size 8 comfortably
* Found me . . . at 130

DEBORAH FEINGOLD, OUTLINE PRESS

JOAN LUNDEN
WORKOUT AMERICA

"If I can do it, you can too."

TIMOTHY WHITE

* Happy, confident, and having fun
* Release my own exercise video
* Still struggling with my weight but managing better as I'm educated about healthy eating
* Up before the sun, making each moment of my day count. I always want to feel this alive.

Chapter 1

IN THE BEGINNING

In your teens, you can toss down those shakes, fries, and greasy burgers — not to mention the pizza — into a seemingly bottomless pit. Then, in your twenties, you find that indiscriminately eating high-fat food starts to catch up with you and stick.

I was never a skinny kid, but I didn't have a weight problem. Even at twenty-seven, when I got married, I weighed about 124 — and I am over five-seven. So I was slim. Sure, I liked my body but didn't give it a second thought. It was just the way I was.

What did it for me was getting pregnant. Going into a first pregnancy, your thoughts turn to the color of the baby's room, cute little outfits, the endless debate over a name. . . . You figure you can gain thirty or forty pounds and bounce right back after you've had the baby. We've all seen those models in the maternity ads: their long shapely legs, their slim hips, and what seems to be a little beach ball stuffed under their shirt. Of course, that's nowhere *near* reality. Getting pregnant changes your body completely.

When I found out I was pregnant, I was thrilled. I just ate indiscriminately, because I wanted to be heavy, I wanted to *look* pregnant! Pregnancy was like this ticket, this automatic permission slip not to have to worry about eating. Pregnancy was a glorious vacation from any obligation to be skinny. If I were ever to do that again — which I'm not going to — I'd approach it in an entirely different way. I would never in a million years gain sixty or seventy pounds.

Of course, like every other patient who visited my obstetrician's office, I was always asked to get on the scale. Talk about added stress! Those mere words shot my blood pressure sky-high, I'm sure, and I became a master at finding excuses for not being weighed. I would say, "Oh, wait a second, I just have to go to the bathroom first." And I'd go in the bathroom and waste time until I'd hear somebody come out of the doctor's office. I would *connive* not to have to get on the scale.

The real problem, though, comes after you've had the baby, when you discover that you still have to lose most of the fifty, sixty, or (oh, please, don't let it be true) seventy pounds gained during pregnancy! That's not how I thought it was going to be. I truly believed that I would gain twenty or thirty pounds, have an eight-pound baby, lose an additional five to ten pounds from giving birth, and have my weight completely under control. Well, ha-ha! Guess the joke was on me!

Now that any resemblance to the body you once knew is gone, how are you supposed to get your weight under control? How are you supposed to run to the gym when you're at home with a newborn? You can't even go for a quick run in the neighborhood, since your breasts are so full and heavy from nursing, you feel they're going to explode. Speaking of nursing, did they tell you that your uterus would contract and miraculously make your stomach flat again? This is some theory . . . right up there with "morning sickness only happens in the morning"!

I don't know about you, but I found myself ravenous after breast-feeding and so unbelievably tired! My uterus may have been contracting, but my fat cells were expanding with every trip to the kitchen for a comforting snack. Now I had a new excuse for eating: to provide nourishment for breast-feeding the baby.

Even though I tried never to get near a scale, I knew how much I weighed. But I couldn't imagine *ever* telling anybody. The thought of admitting to someone what I actually weighed was more than I could bear.

If you went to bed weighing 130 pounds and woke up the next morning weighing 160 pounds, you would probably go into shock and wonder what the heck happened. So why is it so much easier to accept the weight gain when it's gradual? Somewhere, hidden under those sweatpants and baggy tops, was

the driven, fit career woman I once knew. It's hard to get motivated to return to your lean, active old self when you feel overweight, unattractive, undesirable, and just plain overwhelmed by all these new mothering responsibilities. And whoever said the truth hurts must have been doing sit-ups after having a child.

When I finally did make an attempt to lose the weight, I fell into all the traps and tried every extreme, self-depriving diet. I never want to see another rice cake! All you do is set yourself up for failure, because you always fall off these impossible diets and then comfort yourself with food like nachos — at least, I did. I would lose five pounds and gain back seven.

I remember those early years of my career as a blur of invitations and obligations. I had the unfortunate combination of a lot of responsibility and a great need to please everyone. I was one of the first women in the public eye to bring a baby to work, so every major women's magazine wanted to do an article on how I was handling it. I "handled" it by saying yes to every single magazine, not to mention every organization that wanted to "honor me" (meaning I had to show up for the luncheon or dinner and make a speech).

Professionally, I did not know how to say no. I didn't realize the importance of taking time for myself. I know now that if you don't, you pay for it somewhere along the way . . . either in your appearance, your energy level, or your health.

I even said yes to every speech request, despite the fact that speaking in front of a large crowd unnerves me. This always surprises people, given the size of my television audience every day, but television is different. I talk only to a camera, not a room full of people looking back at me!

It was hard enough to deal with a weight problem in the privacy of my own bathroom where I dressed, but add to that a nationwide audience of 25 million people a week. . . . All this visibility, coupled with being new to a network anchor position *and* new to parenthood, was definitely a time of high stress. And by now you know what I did to cope with stress . . . I ate.

I felt a certain hypocrisy being on a show where I was constantly interviewing doctors and telling people how to better their health, and I wasn't following that advice myself. I vividly remember a *Good Morning America* interview with a physician from the American Diabetes Association. As part of the segment, she gave me a diabetes risk test.

AMERICAN DIABETES ASSOCIATION PHYSICIAN:

The risk test was devised to show which individuals are at risk for developing Type II diabetes. And Joan scored high — for a number of reasons. At that point, she was overweight. She did not exercise regularly. And she had a strong family history of diabetes.

It's not just about being skinny. For diabetes and many other health problems, you don't necessarily have to achieve what you might call an "ideal" body weight. Even losing ten pounds is going to improve your outcome. And a long and

healthy life should certainly be a high priority.

Now mind you, diabetes *and* heart attacks run in my family, on both sides. I wasn't particularly interested in setting myself up for them — in fact, I was really scared to death. I wanted to be around when my daughters got married and had kids. What's more, I wanted to feel good enough to do things with them, have fun with them.

Deep down inside, I knew my eating was out of control. I just didn't do anything about it. Well, actually, I did. I became an expert camouflage dresser. Of course, I had the invaluable help of the *Good Morning America* wardrobe consultant, Ellie Dell.

ELLIE DELL:

Although I met Joan over a dozen years ago, she looked and dressed much older than she does now — mostly because she was a much larger size. In a medium like television, you always look bigger than you really are. And heavy people always look better in looser clothes, in things that are actually a little big on them — which is not an easy thing to do, because nobody wants to put on a size 14. If a woman is a full size 12, she'll be damned if she doesn't squeeze into that size 12. Joan would make that mistake.

I got her to wear clothes that were looser on her. The idea was to make her look fabulous but also make her look two sizes smaller than she really was. We would always buy jackets that were nonconstricting, boxier shapes — no belts,

Meeting President Reagan at the White House in 1987

never anything form-fitting. Obviously, that limited the wardrobe, but it produced the desired effect.

We would just be skirting the issue all the time. We'd see clothes that were beautiful, but Joan would say, "Oh, that's not for me," instead of saying, "I'm just too heavy to wear that." It was said, but unsaid.

Over the years, as my weight yo-yo'd up and down, I called upon Ellie Dell many times to rescue me. I remember the first time an envelope arrived with the return address "1600 Pennsylvania Avenue." The White House! I turned it over to check that it was in fact addressed to me. Sure enough, it was. To me, this kind of invitation marked the pinnacle of career success, a fantasy made real. President and Mrs. Reagan had invited *me* to

a dinner honoring the president of El Salvador.

I was so thrilled, I couldn't wait to call my mom. As we talked, Mom asked me, "What are you going to wear?" *What WAS I going to wear?*

To say that sheer panic set in doesn't begin to cover it. I immediately called Ellie. There was an unspoken understanding between us that it was her job to dress me "creatively": to find a dress that would hide my extra weight. I loathed the idea of even having to try on anything.

We eventually found a beautiful Riazzi gold-and-white beaded dress. It was a size 14, and had that large blouson look. It showed absolutely no lines of my figure, so you would have to be Sherlock Holmes himself to know what I was hiding beneath that dress. It reminded me of the kind of dress a larger-sized lounge singer would wear. Actually, I really loved that dress. I just wish it had come with a few thousand less beads!

Sometimes I had to manage without Ellie's help. At photo sessions with magazines, the stylists often provided clothes for me. I'd starve myself beforehand and try to wear black. I used shoulder pads and "big hair" to try to make my face and my body look in proportion.

I always denied what size I really was, which was a huge source of emotion. I had to go with Ellie down to Manhattan's Garment District, walk into all of those designer showrooms, and pretend that I was a size 10. I was *not* a 10.

I might say, "Oh, maybe we ought to get

Wardrobe consultant Ellie Dell (left) with my personal assistant, Jill Alpert, in my dressing room at GMA

that in a twelve, just so it will hang right." And Ellie would call my assistant, Debbie Bergenfeld, and say, "She's not going to fit into these. There isn't a chance in the world she's going to fit into that size." And they would just "up" the size of all the orders and not say anything to me.

The clothes would arrive, and I'd see the sizes. I knew what they had done. It was simply that nobody wanted to acknowledge it. They knew I couldn't bear to talk about it, so we didn't talk about it. They just brought in the sizes that they knew would actually fit me.

In fact, looking back at the time when I was fifty pounds heavier, I am amazed that no one — not my husband, not my agent, not even the producers of *Good Morning America* — ever said to me, "Joan, you've gained some weight. You ought to think about losing a few pounds." How could that be?

DEBBIE BERGENFELD
(personal assistant to Joan Lunden, 1984–92):

Joan really wanted to lose the weight, but she wasn't taking it seriously. We used to go out jogging after the show. We would jog through Central Park and come back to the dressing room and order grilled cheese sandwiches, french fries, milk-shakes. . . . I remember ordering turkey sandwiches on croissants with Swiss cheese and Russian dressing. Once, they forgot the extra Russian dressing on the side, and we made them go back for more.

There were times when people would write in and ask if Joan was pregnant or if she was "hiding good news." I would quickly throw these letters away. I was so overprotective; I didn't want to hurt her feelings, just like everyone else didn't want to hurt her feelings.

Actually, there was one person who brought up the subject — one of the net-

With my former personal assistant Debbie Bergenfeld

work executives — after my second daughter, Lindsay, was born. I came back to work three weeks after I delivered, which was total insanity. On my first day back, the executive made a comment about how I looked too fat and needed to work on getting in shape.

I just exploded. How dare he say this! Here I am, busting my butt to come back three weeks after having a baby, and he's telling me I should weigh less? I was incredibly defensive, because I knew he was right.

And everybody else, of course, jumped on my bandwagon. They didn't want me to feel bad, and they all knew that I was coming back to work way before I should have. This guy got shot down so bad; he was *torpedoed* by every woman in my office. They practically burned him at the stake.

He was the only one who ever said anything. But you know something? It did have an effect on me. It made me aware that other

people were noticing my weight. It made me stop and realize that while I might have just had a baby, there was still a weight issue to contend with. And I did try to lose the weight after that. But I failed. It wasn't until after the third baby that I succeeded.

Now, I know my weight is my own responsibility. I'm not saying, "Gee, nobody ever made me lose weight." I'm just surprised that, even though I worked on television, nobody said anything and that I somehow got away with it. After all, you're supposed to look good on TV — it *is* a visual medium. It sometimes amazes me that I didn't take any flak for those extra pounds. My philosophy at that time was that if I ignored the problem, it didn't exist. While this attitude may have gotten me through some of the roughest times of my life, it wasn't in my best interest. Unfortunately, those skills I developed just served to keep me on my self-destructive track, one seemingly without end.

I was not only overscheduled and exhausted but also unhappy in my marriage. To make it just a bit more stressful, I felt that I couldn't tell anyone, being in the public eye. I felt so alone. Then, too, from outward appearances, I was living the "perfect life." The perception is that a television personality's life is all peaches and cream, as though we never have a problem with weight or with knowing what to wear or what to say at a dinner party. And then there was this "Lucy and Desi" image of the husband-and-wife team happily working together. But we know what happened to Lucille Ball and Desi Arnaz in the end, don't we? You know what they say . . . if it seems too good to be true, it probably is. Somehow, this image had been created — an unrealistic image that was impossible to live up to.

The effects of all this stress were showing not only at work but at home with my family and friends. Bonnie Conklin, my daughters' nanny, witnessed a lot of my down times.

BONNIE CONKLIN:

When I first came to work for Joan, I would see her try to control her weight, but it wasn't a sincere effort. She would try for a little while and then go back to snacking, not really paying much attention to what she ate.

The girls would always eat dinner — because they were younger — before Joan and her husband did. She would sit and eat with them — you know, pick off their plates. And then still eat a meal later.

During the divorce, Joan would come home and make a big pot of Grandma Joie's rice — that's rice with orzo and butter. Or she would open potato chips or some other salty food. That's how I knew when she was really down and depressed.

ELISE SILVESTRI
(Joan's friend and producer of her parenting programming):

My husband, Michael, and I had a standing date with Joan and her husband every Friday night, whether we just went out to dinner or were going to a party somewhere. I always remember being pretty tired myself on Friday nights, but I fig-

ured if Joan can go out after doing *Good Morning America* all week as well as a second show after that, then I certainly could do it.

But there was usually a point during the evening, no matter where we were, when Joan would start to zone out. She was just so bone tired that she physically couldn't keep her eyes open. We could be in the middle of a busy restaurant, and she would start to fall asleep. My husband and I began to take that as our cue to end the evening. I always wondered how long she could keep this up.

I remember one afternoon when I took my three daughters ice-skating at the indoor rink near our home. It was a huge rink, whirling with activity and the sound of muffled music playing over the loudspeaker. I found myself a spot in the bleachers, amidst hundreds of knit caps, book bags, and doting parents watching as their own kids skated by. I watched in awe as children chased each other up and down the bleachers, full of zip after a long day at school. Where did they find so much energy? And why couldn't I tap into some of that?

I didn't skate with my daughters. My maternal responsibility was to watch proudly and wave as they skated by. This was not asking the impossible; but in fact, it was for me. Despite my good intentions, exhaustion overcame me, and I fell fast asleep right there in the bleachers.

I don't know how long I dozed off, but the next thing I remember is one of my daughters persistently shaking me. "Did you see

My youngest daughter, Sarah, in her ice-hockey team uniform

my figure eight, Mom? Did you see it? Did you see it?" Even half-asleep, I couldn't miss her disappointment. Another childhood triumph had passed me by — and right under my nose.

I was going home at night, trying to spend "quality" time with the girls, and practically passing out in the middle of dinner. I would tuck them in at night and try to read a bedtime story; invariably, I was the one asleep before the end. My sense of frustration was growing. I was not in control of my own energy level. I tried to please everyone, forgetting, quite frankly, that I also had to please myself.

How did things get to be this way? Was I facing a lifetime of missing my children's daily achievements? Sure, I could make a million excuses, but not at my children's ex-

pense. My kids are the top priority in my life, and I didn't want to miss one precious moment.

Over ten years and three pregnancies, I grew heavier, unhealthier, and unhappier. Somehow, I wasn't even aware of my downward spiral. All of a sudden something happens, a specific moment in time that smacks you square in the face and wakes you up. It's a rude awakening you never forget, and mine left me hot under the collar — literally.

I was scheduled to compete in a local horse show in Ridgefield, Connecticut. It was definitely one of the hottest days of the summer of 1988 — the kind of heat that makes you perspire the second the humid air hits you. It hadn't rained for weeks, and the horse show fields were especially dusty and dry. Everywhere I looked there were tall, lanky young girls in traditional riding attire: tan riding pants; high-collared, crisp cotton shirts; and dark green and navy jackets. Old customs die hard, even in wilting heat.

Each rider patiently waited to take her turn. I marveled at these young athletes who made it all seem so easy and managed to maintain their composure even in the most extreme of circumstances. I watched my daughter Jamie successfully make her rounds in one division after another.

As my time grew near, I began to really sweat — not just from the heat but also from nervousness. With my crazy schedule, it had been close to a year since I last showed my horse, and my anxiety was almost unbearable. My trainer sent me back to the trailer where we kept all the riding gear. Her trailer was parked in the middle of a grassy field, one among many identical-looking trailers, so familiar at a show like this one.

I went to my trunk and pulled out the items I would need to transform myself from spectator to rider: my riding helmet, traditional outfit, riding gloves, and tall leather boots. I figured I'd change in the front cabin of the trailer. What I didn't figure on was the blast of heat that hit me when I opened the front cabin door. It must have been 110 degrees in there! I was soaked in sweat, and dressing was a challenge.

My real troubles, though, were just beginning. I hadn't attempted to pull my tall leather riding boots over my calves since last year. And you know how your legs can swell on a hot day?

I could hear the announcer calling for all riders in my division to report to the ring. The harder I pulled, the hotter I got, and the surer I was that these boots were *not* going on. Panic set in. "These couldn't be my boots!" I thought to myself. I must have taken Jamie's by mistake. Could I have put on that much weight since last year? What in the world was I going to tell my trainer? I remember hearing myself say, "I've got to get out of this!" There was no way I was walking out of that trailer and telling anyone that I couldn't fit into my boots. Between the sun, the heat, and my nerves, I was an absolute wreck.

I finally did manage to get one boot on — and it completely cut off my circulation. I was certain they would have to cut off my leg with the boot, since there was no room even

to squeeze in a pair of scissors! Now I had no choice. . . . I had to find someone, anyone, who looked strong enough to help get that boot off of me. I opened the trailer door, perused the area, and saw a husky-looking woman standing near a van. I hobbled over, one boot on and the other foot bare, and asked the woman for help.

She gave me a knowing look. Then she proceeded to pull and yank and twist, and then pull some more. She told me to relax my calf muscles. Was she joking? Finally, she managed to separate the boot from my leg.

I remember walking away and sitting under a nearby tree. I had to figure out my next move. I knew I couldn't ride without my boots, and I was too mortified to tell anyone what had happened. As I sat there trying to come up with a decent excuse, I realized what I really needed to do was stop making excuses. The time had come for me to make some changes in my life. In the distance, I heard the announcer of my event give the final results. I would not take a ribbon that day. I had missed my event completely.

This was what my life had come to . . . not quite the perfect picture always portrayed to the public. I couldn't pretend anymore. My reality was that I had no energy. No patience. No ability to wear fashionable clothes. No way to bring down my stress level. No way to stop falling asleep at dinner parties and ice rinks. Any way I added it up, there could no longer be any more excuses for not changing my life.

This time I'm going to make it work. . . . The start of my journey.

Chapter 2

✢

N O   M O R E   E X C U S E S !

When I started researching and reminiscing for this book, I asked my assistant, Samantha Berg, to look at tapes of the January 1 *Good Morning America* shows for the past fifteen years. Every year we talk about our New Year's resolutions. And every year until 1990, my resolution was the same: I wanted to lose weight and get into shape. What a surprise!

It still amazes me to recall how I looked, how stressed out I was, and how much I constantly talked about wanting to lose weight — but didn't do it. What finally "tipped the scales" for me was facing the calendar.

Some people get all wigged out over their thirtieth, fortieth, or fiftieth birthday. For me, it was my thirty-ninth. As that day of reckoning drew near, I was reading all those "fabulous at forty" articles in the women's magazines. Jane Fonda, Jackie Bissett, Farrah Fawcett . . . I wanted to be in that "fabulous" company!

The combination of too many humiliating memories (especially the horse show disaster) and the feeling that time was slipping away made me finally face the truth about myself. I knew I had two choices: I could turn forty and be overweight, continue to feel and look crummy, and be depressed about it. Or I could get in shape, lose the weight, and gain back my self-esteem. I could turn forty looking good, feeling good, and knowing that I would spend the next forty years as an active, fun-loving, fun-to-be-with person.

This was what you call a no-brainer: I knew what my choice had to be. I just had to figure out how to do it — and how to get started. I decided that I would give myself one year to get it together. Each day would be part of a countdown to forty. I went on the attack against the march of time.

I announced to everyone that this time I was going to get in shape. Spencer Christian, my friend and co-worker on *Good Morning America,* is extremely fit and health-conscious. He'd heard me talk for so long about wanting to lose weight.

SPENCER CHRISTIAN:

In my mind, I was saying, "Then just do something about it! You have to change your eating habits, and you have to exercise." But it was really hard for me to say that, because I didn't want to hurt Joan's feelings.

Charlie (left), Spencer, and me on location for GMA *in St. Croix*

It was in early 1988 when I started working up the courage to finally say something. We had done two shows in the Virgin Islands.

As we finished up the second day's broadcast on St. Thomas, we all had to board a seaplane to go over to St. Croix. And one of the requirements for boarding a seaplane is that after going through the ticketing process, everyone has to be weighed.

I noticed that Joan didn't want to get on the scales with everybody else around. I knew the reason: she didn't want anyone to see how much she weighed.

I felt so bad for her, because it wasn't just Charlie Gibson and me there with her, but also a couple of the show's producers. I knew she must have felt so awful at that moment.

The boarding agent said, "I'm sorry, ma'am, but it's a regulation required by the air service. You must get on the scales." So she did. And I said to myself then, "I'm going to have to tell her that she's got to do something about her weight."

Not too long after our trip to the Caribbean, we had to hit the road again — this time, we were leaving for the 1988 Democratic National Convention in Atlanta. I was struggling with my wardrobe for the convention, vowing for the umpteenth time that I needed to lose a few pounds. Finally, Spencer told me, "Stop talking about losing weight. Get up off your butt and *do* something about it already!" "All right," I said, "I will." And somehow, I really meant it. I'm not sure how I knew, but I was convinced that I was going to make it work.

The first thing I did when I checked into my room at the hotel was scan the room service menu. I was determined not to fall prey to the temptations of late-night hotel-room snacking on high-fat, high-calorie munchies. Instead, I looked for the low-fat items that I thought would be smart choices for me.

I managed to bypass the nachos with cheddar cheese and the potato skins with sour cream and bacon, but I didn't want to be tempted more than once. I compiled a list of acceptable food choices, walked that room service menu down the hall, and left it on top of the credenza by the elevator. For the next week, I would never have to see the words "with extra guacamole and sour cream" again.

Additionally, Spencer agreed that he would be my workout buddy. When the show was finished each day, I donned my exercise clothes and met Spencer at the hotel gym. The first day I tried the exercise bike . . . and hated it. While Spencer could easily pedal for thirty minutes, *five* minutes seemed hard to me. But let's face it, after not working out for some twenty years, anything would have been hard. You have to start somewhere.

Being a workout buddy means keeping your partner motivated, and that's just what Spencer did for me. He wouldn't let me give up. He encouraged me to try another machine, something that would hold my interest. Spencer helped me realize that it would get easier, as long as I stuck with the program.

SPENCER CHRISTIAN:
I think that I just about dragged her there the first day, to make sure she went. But

she did go, every day. She just got into the rhythm of working out for that week. And I said to myself, "I wonder if she'll stay with it."

When I returned home from that trip, I was amazed and thrilled to find that I'd dropped six pounds. I could hardly contain my excitement. Seeing positive results is definitely the best motivation to continue on a weight-loss program.

In the past, I had always gained weight on the road. Losing weight was new and exciting for me. But how in the world was I going to transfer this success to my everyday routine at home? I was, after all, returning to a house filled with young children, macaroni and cheese, sloppy joes, and cream-filled cookies. Fortunately, before I (once again) grew discouraged and gave up, I was off on my next assignment: the Republican National Convention in New Orleans.

Proud of myself, I repeated my room service ritual. But I had just one small problem . . . this hotel had no gym! Once again, it was Spencer to the rescue. A few blocks from our hotel he found a well-equipped gym that we could walk to after the show each day. This was great but posed one more dilemma for me: the combination of my fifty extra pounds, a leotard, and a public gym. See where I'm going here?

Working out in a public gym was one of my biggest obstacles for years. I was the customer most gyms wait for: I always paid my fees and never used the facility. For me, public scrutiny was a major deterrent. I never wanted to be one of those women I saw at the gym who were poured into their leotards, saddlebags and all . . . you know, the ones you look at and hope you don't resemble? I surely did not want a zillion strangers looking at me, all out of shape and pretending I knew what I was doing every time I tried to get the treadmill started.

But I didn't want to lose that momentum now! I dug up an oversized T-shirt and some dark-colored leggings, and off I went. With every ounce I lost, I gained much-needed self-esteem. I forced myself to learn to deal with these types of dilemmas and finally began my journey to fitness. To this day, I thank Spencer for making me go to that public gym, as hard as it was.

In the fall of 1988, my executive producer, Jack Reilly, noticed that I was losing weight. Pleased that I was finally taking the initiative to trim down, he suggested sending me to a spa to do a special segment for *Good Morning America.* I had actually thought of this idea before but didn't follow through on it, because I still felt too heavy to be seen in sweats or, God forbid, a leotard. Or swathed in a very large terry cloth towel, covered in a seaweed wrap . . . I was really looking forward to this — sure, over my big, fat dead body!

But I finally agreed to don all of that exercise gear and go for it — in public. This assignment made me even more determined to stick with my program, so I could look as good as possible before I got there . . . kind of like cleaning the house before a housekeeper comes.

I spent one week at the Doral spa in Florida in November 1988. I came home down another six or seven pounds. I was finally getting the picture that running to keep up with my busy schedule was a far cry from working out in the gym.

I returned from the Doral totally motivated to stay on this track of fitness and weight loss. Ideally, I wanted to have a workout buddy. Unfortunately, I found that my schedule didn't allow me to get together regularly with anyone.

Luckily, soon after my return from the spa, I went to the home of Barbara Brandt to pick up my daughter Lindsay from a playdate with Barbara's daughter. It was there that I learned that Barbara, who had been right under my nose, was a personal fitness trainer. We resolved that after the holidays, we would start 1989, my thirty-ninth year, with a personalized fitness program. Up to that point, I had really only been concerned with losing weight. For the first time I found myself also interested in total fitness. Barbara would give me a *fitness consciousness.*

BARBARA BRANDT:
There's a certain vulnerability when people come to me as a fitness trainer. It doesn't matter how rich they are or how famous. When they're standing there with just a thin layer of clothing on, it's as if I, as a trainer, can see through them. I can see through to what it is they are having to deal with.

When I met Joan, she was a person who was not physical. Even if somebody goes to a spa or does something active on the weekend, I really don't consider that being physical, because it's inconsistent. So I really had to start with her from scratch, from the ground up.

There was definitely a discrepancy between what I saw in Joan and what her goals were. Joan saw herself as a person who had to take off weight and get into shape. What I saw was a person who needed to work on food issues as well as weight issues — all the emotional issues that are associated with food, including the stress of an overwhelming schedule, a rocky marriage, and how all of that affects your eating.

For many women, food is a real issue. They are the nurturers, yet sometimes they don't take the time to nurture themselves.

So you use food to nurture yourself, and you put on weight and feel crummy about it. Then you eat more because it soothes you. Then you start to think, "My God, what did I do? I just downed a pint of ice cream!" It creates a vicious cycle.

I learned right away that Joan was a very driven person. One of my goals for Joan was for her to learn that results can't be gotten immediately. Quick fixes don't last and don't work. You can injure yourself by overexercising. You can mess up your metabolism by dieting too strenuously. So my goal was to offer her exercise with moderation. Her goal was to take off fifty pounds yesterday and be able to get into a different size tomorrow!

Here she was, a very established celebrity, having paid her dues in her career.

Because she was getting such great results in one aspect of her life, she didn't understand why she wouldn't get the same results immediately in other areas.

Our propensity for instant gratification can be a frustration when working out and dieting, but as my friend and chiropractor Dr. Sam Schwartz once said to me, "It took you ten years and three pregnancies to gain all of this weight. What makes you think you can lose it in two months?" Food for thought . . .

I went through a period when I weighed myself all the time, to check my progress. I don't need to get on a scale now; I can get up and look at myself and know where I'm at, because I've become conscious of my own state of fitness. I can tell even before I look in the mirror, just by the way I feel. I never used to be able to do that. I spent a lot of time ignoring my body.

SPENCER CHRISTIAN:

I've noticed that Joan seems to be the kind of person who, when she tries something new, after the initial experience of getting over the awkwardness, develops a feeling of comfort and really throws herself into it. And that's exactly what she did with exercising. It didn't take her very long at all to just start charging full speed ahead.

While some people might have viewed that as compulsiveness or obsessiveness, I didn't. I thought it was just a great thing. I could see her self-esteem growing. I could see Joan developing a better

Feeling like a million bucks . . .

feeling about herself daily and weekly. You could see this new person emerging.

MARK DANIEL FONZI *(Joan's hair stylist):*

When Joan was heavier, she always wanted her hair big and full, so that it would be in proportion to her body. When she became so fit and trim, I wanted to give her a whole new look that would match her new personality. It was amazing how much younger she looked when I cut her hair short. I never dreamed it would have gotten so much media attention; people are still talking about it. It was a bold move, and something she would never have done before she lost weight.

MICHELLE CUTLER *(Joan's makeup artist):*

The more weight Joan lost, the less makeup she needed. She always had a beautiful face, but we used to have to create her features with shading. Today, she has great cheekbones and a slim, more chiseled face. It's a perfect canvas for a makeup artist to work on.

One thing that really kept me going was all the support I got from friends and fans. It was quite endearing that everybody was so behind me. I'd go through airports, and people would yell, "Hey, Joan! Right on! Looking great!"

BARBARA BRANDT:

As Joan blossomed, her posture changed along with her self-esteem. Posture is really about presentation. It's not just about whether your stomach muscles or your back muscles are strong. It's a matter of whether you're also willing to stand up straight and present yourself and be looked at. And if you're fifty pounds overweight and don't feel good about yourself physically, then you're not going to do that.

One of the most exciting aspects of my weight loss was recognizing all the other benefits. My skin was clearer, my eyes were brighter — I felt stronger, healthier, and more energetic. I woke up one morning and somehow just knew that I was going to be all right. I knew that I was no longer in fear of living my life as an overweight, unhappy, un-

Hair stylist Mark Daniel Fonzi and makeup artist Michelle Cutler put some finishing touches on me.

healthy woman. It was like a door had been opened to my soul. The realization itself was like losing fifty pounds.

What's more, I was starting to believe that I deserved to feel this good. A time will come in your own weight loss when you can say to yourself, "Aha! *This* is how I'm supposed to feel." What a great moment that will be for you.

SAMANTHA BERG
(personal assistant to Joan, 1992–95):

Joan's self-esteem has grown tremendously. She's a lot freer with herself. She always amazes me because she can focus and work so hard but also can let go and relax and have a great time with the crew, especially when we're on the road. When we go on our bus trips, Joan's bus has the fabulous disco tapes blaring, and we all dance for hours. And there's Joan right there in the middle of the *GMA* staff,

never sitting still for a moment, making sure everyone is having a good time.

I also notice that people in the office are nervous to ask whether Joan would be willing to do physical activities for the show. I remember one time they wanted her to ice-skate with Olympic champion Brian Boitano. And Joan said, "Of course I'll do it. How cool!" The producer, who had been there for a long time, was really surprised. Because he did not think Joan would be able — let alone be willing — to do the segment, based on her history. But today, when she hears about people going on bike trips or climbing mountains, she says to the producer, "Hey, send *me* on one of those. How about Mount McKinley?" Before, she never would have done that in a million years. I think at the beginning of her weight loss, she didn't realize that those kinds of things were within her reach or that she'd ever even want to do them.

With my former personal assistant, Samantha Berg, on Catalina Island for a Dick Clark special for ABC television

As I continued to come down in weight, other great milestones were achieved. For example, I began giving away all my big clothes, because I didn't want to have them around to grow back into again. I used to always have a wardrobe of some easy-fitting 10s, 12s, 14s — I don't want to mention any other sizes!

I don't have a wardrobe like that anymore.

I do give myself some slack, but I don't allow myself to get out of control. If I'm not fitting into my 8s comfortably, I know that I need to be paying a little closer attention. I don't kick myself if I'm not fitting into my tightest jeans. But I do hang them prominently in my closet, so I can see them and want them.

DEBBIE BERGENFELD
(personal assistant to Joan, 1984–92):

The Joan of today is much more easygoing than when I worked for her. I think she lets things roll off her back a lot more. I think her self-esteem has gotten so much better. I see a much more fun, loving Joan. I see a much calmer Joan. She's able to laugh at herself. Joan loves to laugh, and she did so little laughing before, because of her low self-esteem and being in a bad marriage.

I'll never forget her first photo session after she lost all her weight. It was with the famous fashion photographer Timothy White at his studio. After we finished, she wanted some fun shots. She grabbed one of his jackets out of his closet and put it over a little sexy black dress. We went up on the roof of his building, and he shot the best pictures that I had ever seen of her. She was posing and finally feeling good about herself. It was one of the most successful photo shoots I have ever seen her do.

It's not just about taking great pictures, or fitting into those tight jeans and looking good in them. Wearing a smaller size is just a perk of losing weight. The real benefits are far more important. It's a responsibility we all

For the first time in years, I actually enjoyed this photo session.

lowed a guest doctor to test my cholesterol and announce my results live on the air. I knew that one of the benefits of all my working out was that I didn't have to be afraid of what she would find.

The results turned out to be amazing! The doctor found that I had substantially lowered my cholesterol level. I knew that I felt good, but I hadn't realized just how far I had come in improving my health.

I mentioned before how worried I was when that doctor from the American Diabetes Association told me I was at high risk for developing the disease they call "the silent killer." I remember the words so clearly from back then: "Of the almost fourteen million Americans who have diabetes, nearly half don't know it." I was scared to death that I was one of those 14 million.

When Dr. Kathleen Wishner, a past director of the American Diabetes Association, visited *Good Morning America* in May 1995, I retook the test and saw that by changing my life, I had changed my health risks. The same quiz that once classified me as high-risk now showed I had nothing to worry about. In fact, the doctor said, "You are walking proof that we all have control over our health."

Remember all of those New Year's resolutions to start dieting and exercising? My New Year's resolution in 1990, after my yearlong journey to fitness, was to "start having half as much fun as the newspapers say I have."

It's so nice to finally live up to my New Year's resolutions.

have to our own bodies, to be in the best health we can.

Although I often interview doctors on *Good Morning America,* I never used to let them give me medical tests, as I was absolutely terrified of the results. Now, in my new fit condition, for the first time ever I al-

Chapter 3

YOU'VE GOT TO EAT TO LIVE

When I was a little girl, I remember my mom used to say that some people eat to live, but she lives to eat. Well, it always got a laugh, but there's some real truth in what she said. You do have to eat to live. The idea is to combine a love of eating with healthy choices. Maybe that's the most important thing I have learned on this journey, that you can't diet all your life. Weight control is not about starvation. It's learning how to live with food and how to make the right choices. That's why I find myself writing a cookbook rather than a diet book.

Most people give very little consideration to the food choices they make. I don't know why. We consider the other daily decisions in our life important: choosing a job, a house, our friends, our clothes. You wouldn't just indiscriminately throw something on your body and go out: you think about what you're going to wear. So why do we consider our food choices any less worthy of some thought and planning? It's our health, our body — what could be more important? And yet, I was never consciously aware that I was making choices. I was just a gatherer and consumer of food.

Food shouldn't be an enemy. You must have a healthy relationship with food. And don't fear that in order to keep weight off, you have to starve yourself to death. That's such a myth. There are so many wonderful foods and delicious dishes you can eat that are healthy, will fill you up, and will give you tremendous enjoyment. It's a matter of taking the time to find foods that you like and that also happen to be good for you.

I know there are people — I used to be one — who say, "I don't like vegetables," or "I don't like fruit," but have tried only one or two things. They haven't really looked into the wide range of low-fat, healthful, tasty stuff that's out there. In this chapter, I pass on my favorite tips from the top experts who helped me completely change the way I eat, cook, and think about food.

The Food Diary

Nutrition was the area where my knowledge was weakest. To fill that gap, I made an appointment with famed nutritionist Hermiene Lee. The first thing she had me do was to start keeping a food diary. I would never have been able to predict how enlightening

Me dancing in a parade when I was ten years old

Me modeling in a fashion show at age nine

this seemingly trivial task would be. To me, it looked like just busywork.

But Hermiene wanted to open my eyes to what I ate from the moment I woke up in the morning until the minute my head hit the pillow at night. I needed to be aware of when I was eating, where I was eating, and what I was eating. Once I started keeping this journal, I was shocked to see just what my eating habits were.

I was told to write in the food diary not only everything I ate on a particular day but also such things as:

- the times I got hungry
- where I was and what I was doing when I got hungry or had a particular craving
- what I was thinking or feeling when I got hungry
- what I thought my eating choices were, and what my frustrations were
- what I ended up eating
- when and where I ate (e.g., standing at the fridge, sitting in front of the TV)
- how I felt after I ate (e.g., was I angry at myself for my choice)

I learned a lot from my food journal. For

starters, I didn't realize I ate as much as I did. And I didn't realize I ate so unconsciously. Because my day starts at 4:00 A.M., I found that by the time I got off the air at 9:00 A.M., I was hungry again. That would equal no less than two breakfasts. By noon, it was time for lunch. And when I brought my kids home from school, I would find my energy level again at a low point, and again would indulge. All too often, the girls just couldn't wait until their father got home for dinner, so I would end up sitting down with them around 6:00 P.M., and again when he got home around 8:00. According to my calculations, that's at least six meals a day. I had no idea what I was doing until I read it in black and white. No wonder I had a weight problem!

Reviewing my food journal allowed Hermiene to say, "This is what you're doing to yourself, these are what your problems are, these are your vulnerable times. You have traps in your life, and you're falling into them — you're getting sucked right in."

Once I started tracking my patterns, I was better able to plan my meals and deal with my "in-between" desires. Keeping a food journal helps you find out what your downfalls are, your weak points during the day, and where your willpower is failing you. So, why keep testing yourself? I'm not good at having my willpower tested over and over again. I have learned to eliminate those situations as much as possible.

When *Good Morning America* is done for the day, I feel like I do when a big party I've planned is over. There's a bit of a letdown.

My energy level is low, my blood sugar is low, and I feel like I need a pick-me-up. The food diary helped me see that this was an absolute time of weakness for me. At the time, eating would always make me feel better, but the choices I was making were killing me.

Hermiene suggested keeping a small refrigerator in my dressing room, and stocking it with fresh fruit, nonfat milk and yogurt, and nonfat cheese. She also suggested that I keep some healthy snacks that would satisfy my need to "crunch," as well as some small boxes of healthy cereal. I chose shredded wheat, since it has no fat, no sugar, and no salt. Now, when I get off the air, I know I have healthy snacks waiting — not the doughnuts and Danishes provided by the show, which used to be my only choices.

It's quite common to have doughnuts and coffee cake around a set. But a funny thing happened at *Good Morning America* when I started to change my diet. I encouraged our catering department to start bringing fresh fruit and bagels instead. At first, I thought there was going to be a mutiny. And, in fact, there were a few members of the staff (and you know who you are) who were upset. But most were happy with the change. Now, we have a tasty selection of fresh fruit, nonfat yogurt, cereal with skim milk, low-fat muffins, and bagels.

Eat Food You Like

The important thing is to be realistic in your selections, to feel as though you've really eaten something and have satisfied your particular desire. Otherwise, it's inevitable that you're just going to eat what you really want later.

Hermiene stressed the importance of eating foods you like, not just the foods you think you're supposed to eat to lose weight. For example, I told her that I hated water-packed tuna. Her response was, "Why eat it, then?" Deprivation will only lead to cheating. Hermiene believes and has taught me that it's okay to eat the foods you want — but in moderation and, if possible, in lower-fat versions.

In this book, I have recipes for unfried french fries, potato skins — all the things that I love. I've just learned how to make them by reducing the fat. I adore Mexican food, and I can still eat quesadillas: I just use nonfat cheese and nonfat sour cream now. On occasion, I even prepare a reduced-fat guacamole (one of my favorites), and top off my quesadilla with it! I am totally satisfied by the taste and don't feel deprived. Every now and then, you have to treat yourself. If you don't, you'll just set yourself up for failure.

If I get a turkey sandwich with tomatoes and lettuce, and want Russian dressing — and sometimes I do — I get it on the side. I take a little bit of dressing, put it on a few bites of sandwich, and feel that I've had what I really wanted.

If you don't eat something you really like, you will eat again. I made that mistake for a long time. I ordered all the "shoulds": the cottage cheese, the rice cakes. Two hours later

I would be hungry again; and I would be so mad at myself, because I never satisfied my cravings.

I learned you can't eat just whatever is on some list of "approved" foods. You need to go back to your doctor or dietician and say, "I don't need this general list of celery sticks, carrot sticks, and water-packed tuna, because I hate those things. It's totally unrealistic, and I'm not eating that." You have to discover what the foods are that *you* like and that are okay to eat. We all need *that* list.

I told Hermiene that I don't really like fruit in the morning, because it's too acidic for me. I need some kind of a bread product in my stomach. So she said, "Go get a bagel, scoop out the dough, and fill the crust with nonfat cheese. Maybe put a little slice of tomato or salsa on it. Then put it in the toaster oven. Now, you'll really feel like you had a meal."

Weight loss is not about deprivation. We all live in the real world, and I am sure that, like me, you will constantly be faced with making real-world choices. Techniques for making these choices are what Hermiene taught me.

A New Attitude: No More "Bad" and "Good"

My attitude about food today is so much better than it used to be. I am much more in control of what I eat and how much I eat. I needed to learn to eat like a child again. A toddler knows when she's hungry and when she's not, and she listens to her body. When she's full, she stops eating.

Part of this process is a total reconditioning of the way you think about and react to food. How you think about food determines your attitude toward eating, dieting, and losing weight, so your success hinges on having a healthy perspective on these things. It's as much psychological as it is physical.

When you start a weight-loss program, you have to be realistic in your expectations, setting small goals that are attainable. Staying motivated plays a large part in whether you are successful. One suggestion is to get beyond the focus on becoming a smaller size, and to realize the broader implications of losing weight. It is within your power to control your energy level and to improve your health, just by making different choices about what you eat. You can significantly reduce your risk of major health problems, such as heart disease, cancer, high blood pressure, diabetes . . . I could go on and on. It's not just about looking good — it's about feeling better and living longer.

A hurdle I had to get over in order to establish a healthy relationship with food was to stop using "bad" and "good" to describe my eating habits. I used to say, "I was 'bad' today because I had cake and ice cream at the office party," or "I was 'good' today because I ate only dry tuna for lunch." Feeling bad is a natural setup for feeling guilty and for saying, "To hell with it. I've already screwed up today, so what's the difference?" It's one of the quintessential traps.

Both Hermiene Lee and my fitness trainer,

Barbara Brandt, would constantly remind me that the concept of "bad" and "good" foods is self-defeating. Instead, tell yourself that you had that cake and ice cream, you enjoyed it, and you'll balance it by skipping dessert at dinner or doing an extra fifteen minutes on the treadmill.

Eat Slowly and Enjoy

Eating is as much a habit as it is a necessity. Identifying the difference is the secret. I am what some experts would call an "unconscious eater." I would eat because it felt good, it was comforting, and I liked the crunch. I just wasn't aware of how much I was eating or how quickly I was eating.

I was amazed when my nutritionist pointed out, "You finished this whole meal in six minutes!" Experts say that once food reaches your stomach, it takes about twenty minutes before your brain gets the signal that you're not hungry anymore.

Hermiene taught me tricks to slow down my eating. She had me take a bit of salad and dunk it into a few drops of dressing. She said to chew that bite completely before I put my fork back into the bowl for another taste. I became acutely aware of eating and enjoying each separate bite.

Eating slowly and consciously is still a challenge for me. It's hard to break old habits. But now I know that if I slow down my food intake, I'll find that I don't need nearly as much food as is served in a typical portion. Try cutting a bagel into thin slices. Toast the slices and eat them slowly; I swear that you'll eat one-fourth of a bagel and think you just ate the whole thing.

Getting It

I had shed over twenty-five pounds when I hit a plateau in my weight loss. I turned to Dr. Sam Schwartz, a holistic doctor of chiropractic whom I had been to many times for chiropractic therapy and who has helped many of my friends in the area of nutrition. He really helped me to get beyond my plateau. He explained to me that it's not unusual to hit a point where you just stop losing weight, as your body gets used to regular exercise and reduced food intake. When your body sees this new state as "normal," you can maintain the weight you're at, but it gets much harder to keep losing.

Dr. Schwartz recommended that I go on the Duke University rice-and-fruit diet. It is quite a strict program that should be followed *only* under a doctor's care. You must supplement the diet with essential vitamins and nutrients, and it is of the utmost importance that a professional monitor your progress.

The rice-and-fruit diet consists of a portion of fruit in the morning, and two fruits plus three-quarters of a cup of cooked brown rice for lunch and dinner. For me, this program was a real turning point. I used to think that if I did not have a certain amount of food, I would get headaches and feel hungry all the time. I thought that I would have no energy. I was sure that I could never make it through my day without all that food.

Lo and behold, this diet proved me wrong. To my surprise, I did not feel any of those negative effects. That was an incredible discovery for me. I'd walk into Sam Schwartz's office, and he'd ask me how I felt.

I felt incredibly great. I felt so healthy and vibrant!

Sam would smile knowingly and ask, "Well, are you getting it, that you didn't need those quantities of all that salt-laden food in order to feel good and energetic and not headachy?"

After being on the rice diet for a few weeks, I felt I'd cleansed my system. I'd completely eliminated fat, sodium, caffeine, and food preservatives from my diet. This "detoxing" period had tremendous benefits for me. My makeup artist noticed that my skin was clearer. For the first time, I was aware that I was affecting the way my body was operating. I was in control. What a trip! It felt great.

After the Duke plan, Sam slowly started introducing vegetables into my diet. First, he had me cook and eat a plain zucchini. With that first bite, I thought, "My God, zucchini has a flavor!" I had never eaten a zucchini without butter and salt before. I discovered the taste of food! I never knew so many foods tasted so good not covered with cream sauce, salt, and butter.

I also learned how to make healthy sauces using tomato, onion, and green pepper. I don't cook with butter and salt anymore. I used to use them indiscriminately, because everybody did. If most people just cut the butter, salt, and extra fat out of their diet, they'd be down five pounds before they knew what happened. Instead of butter and salt, add some herbs. Bingo, you've got flavor! And it's food that you actually like.

Sam had been asking me for a long time if I was "getting it." I never understood his question until I went on this diet. Finally, I realized that I did "get it." I didn't need mass quantities of food to live and be happy. That's "it." You must "get it" if you're going to lose weight and keep it off. Once you understand this basic principle, losing weight just seems to get easier. I lost a total of eighteen pounds with this diet. I literally reconditioned the way I thought about food.

In fact, the Duke regimen even helped me break my habit of drinking diet soda. The rice-and-fruit diet didn't allow diet soda, since most are filled with caffeine and salt. I started drinking more water, as well as mixing fruit juices with water. Once again, since I'm not a believer in deprivation, I'll admit that I do drink a Diet Coke every now and then, but I don't live on it anymore.

So when all was said and done, I'd gotten used to eating smaller portions of food, gotten past my plateau, and reached a whole new level in my weight loss. This was all unbelievably exciting. While the rice-and-fruit diet is not for everyone, nor will I tell you that it's the easiest diet, it worked for me.

Healthy Shopping

What you keep in your kitchen determines what you're cooking, what you're eating, and how well you're eating. It starts with how you shop and what you buy at the grocery store.

I am now a 100 percent different shopper. I used to shop indiscriminately: this looks good, throw it in the basket. Now, I read every single food label. In fact, I'll probably read three of them before I'll decide which brand is right. It took some time to learn that while one product may have a few more calories, it may have less fat and less sodium, and therefore is a better choice for me. This takes comparative shopping.

According to health reporter Jane Brody, author of *Jane Brody's Good Food Book,* only 20 to 30 percent of your calories should come from fat — but the typical American eats the fat equivalent of a stick of butter a day! Nutritionists say we only need about 220 milligrams of sodium per day; about half a teaspoon does the job, but most of us take in the equivalent of two to four teaspoons. One of my problems is that I retain water when I eat a lot of sodium, so it was crucial to my weight loss to reduce my sodium intake. Know what you're buying, and understand the labels. Once armed with this knowledge, you can make the right choices for you and your family.

Simply choosing low-fat or nonfat products when they're available can really add up to a big difference. For example, in the dairy department, I used to buy 2 percent, the so-called low-fat milk. Then I learned how many grams of fat you lose by switching to 1 percent or skim milk. Skim milk contains 5 percent calories from fat per cup, and 1 percent milk contains 23 percent calories from fat per cup. But 2 percent milk jumps up to 35 percent calories from fat per cup, and whole milk has 49 percent calories from fat per cup — that's quite a change. Interestingly enough, despite its name, buttermilk contains only 20 percent of calories from fat per cup. Of course, "reduced-fat" doesn't mean no calories, so I'm always careful. Read your labels.

I've also found that now when I grocery shop, I "think fresh." No, this doesn't mean that I meet men in the produce department! It means that I buy lots of fresh vegetables like carrots, cucumbers, tomatoes, lettuce, red and green peppers, and onions. I also like to use fresh herbs when I cook, so I keep fresh basil, rosemary, and thyme. I even keep fresh garlic around, which is not one of my favorites, but I use it sparingly to enhance flavor.

Sometimes when I come home at the end of the day, I've got to have something to munch on. So I buy all kinds of low-fat munchies with interesting flavors, like no-fat cracked pepper flatbreads. I fill my refrigerator with cut-up fruit ready to be eaten, cut-up vegetables ready to put into the steamer, and fresh turkey every week. I learned to like all kinds of new fruits, especially papaya. Today, when I walk into my house, I know where I can get a quick, healthy snack that will leave me satisfied.

Healthy Eating with Your Family

It's very important to discuss your intentions with family and friends when starting a weight-loss program. But don't assume that

they'll go on it with you. That's unrealistic and may result in resentment or, worse, sabotage. However, if you can make them understand how important this is to you, they'll be more apt to become a support system and spare you the temptation of fattening treats. You never know . . . you may even influence them by your example.

I was always very conscious that while I was watching my diet, my three girls were watching it, too. I wanted them to know that I was choosing a healthy lifestyle, not just dieting. It was important to me to instill in them at an early age the habits of eating right and keeping active.

I know that I'm setting a good example by taking care of myself. I hope they've learned that taking care of themselves should be a priority in their lives. They also see how a healthy diet and regular exercise program help make me a less frazzled parent — and a heck of a lot more fun to be with.

With the children, the real test for me is buying treats for them — the occasional chips, cookies, or frozen yogurt. Luckily, sweets aren't a real temptation for me, but a good tortilla chip or potato chip will always call out my name.

My girls have benefited from the changes I've made in the way I shop and cook, because my cupboards aren't stocked with sodium-filled, fat-laden, sugar-loaded junk. But I don't think kids should be made to feel totally deprived of the kinds of food some of their friends eat. Believe me, we make some trade-offs. For example, I used to let my girls have any kind of breakfast cereal they wanted

Me and my girls at the Pocahontas *premiere in Central Park, June 1995*

in the morning. We have now come to a compromise, where they must eat a low-sugar cereal like shredded wheat, Grape Nuts, or Special K during the week. On the weekends, they can have any cereal they choose.

Another example: I don't deprive the kids of mashed potatoes, I just don't fill them full of cream, salt, and butter, the way my mom likes them. During a recent visit, Mom was just totally aghast to hear that I made mashed potatoes with *skim milk!* Well, I compro-

mised with her and used 1 percent instead, plus a tiny bit of butter.

I have one child who is totally vegetarian: no meat, no fish, no chicken, no eggs. That presented me with a whole new creative challenge. I had to buy books and educate myself. As with a lot of teenagers, her initial approach was just to stop eating that stuff, eliminating animal protein from her diet completely. As a parent, my responsibility is to teach her how to put protein back into her diet: pairing beans with rice or putting tofu into the stir-fry to make a complete protein. But her decision to practice vegetarianism has also helped me, by cutting down the amount of meat I eat.

Healthy Eating in Restaurants

I was lucky in that when I was ready to lose weight and get fit, Americans in general were becoming more aware of what they ate. I can go to a restaurant today and find low-fat choices on the menu quite easily. It used to be that I had to call ahead and prearrange my meals with a restaurant, which often was embarrassing for me. It meant everyone knew that I was dieting, and I felt scrutinized and judged if I ate an extra piece of bread.

One thing I did learn, though, is that most restaurants are only too happy to accommodate you. If you do call ahead, you can get a low-fat, healthy meal. Eating out is not an excuse for tossing aside your healthy habits. Try not to use it as one, and plan ahead.

When I know that I'm eating out, I go to

places that I am sure offer choices of foods that I like and that fit my lifestyle. I look for restaurants that offer pasta, fresh fish, fresh vegetable dishes, or healthy chicken dishes. All restaurants can grill a piece of chicken or fish without butter or heavy sauces. You just have to know that you can ask them to do it for you. In fact, when I was on my rice-and-fruit diet, I would go so far as to tell them that I was deathly allergic to butter and salt and that if they put any in at all, they would certainly be calling 911 before the end of the evening.

You don't have to go to that extreme, but don't be afraid to ask for what you want. I love having breakfast after the show at an outdoor café near the studio. My favorite dish on the menu is a tomato, mozzarella, and pesto omelette. These days I have no problem saying to the server, "I'm not big on pesto, and I don't want the omelette cooked in oil. Can I get a minute amount of mozzarella, lots of tomato . . . and can you make it with just egg whites? And will you please tell them not to use salt?" The restaurant gets a happy and loyal customer, I get a delicious omelette, and best of all, I don't have to do an extra hour on the treadmill.

I also ask servers to skip the high-fat side dishes — no focaccia bread or hash brown potatoes, please, just a piece of rye toast. Why? Because if it's on the plate, you're probably going to eat at least half of it.

What's going to be the thing on the table that will be hardest to pass up? Well, do your damnedest not to get it on the table! And if it is there, have two bites. If they bring nachos because someone at your table has ordered them, just have a couple, and discreetly move the plate away from you. You can't ask to have everything taken away when you're eating with other people.

Healthy Traveling

Now when I fly, I call the airline ahead of time and order a fresh fruit plate. Why eat that fattening airline food if you don't have to? I told my travel agent, "Don't ever put me on a flight without a fruit plate."

When I get on a plane, I say to the flight attendant, "No nuts and no cookies. I want only my fruit plate. And I don't want to see that hot fudge sundae you guys bring around — please don't ask me if I want it!" And they honor that.

When I go on the road with *Good Morning America,* I may be trapped on a bus for five days. People give us goodies they've baked, the crew comes on the bus with bags of potato chips: I know I won't be able to resist everything, and I'd be an unhappy person if I did.

So at times I tell myself, I know I'm probably going to gain five pounds on this trip. I know it from past experience and from my knowledge of how I can't test my willpower every second of the day. And I don't want to beat myself up for it. I'm going to consider this a normal part of life. I'm going to come back home, step up the time I work out a little bit, and take the weight off; life will go on.

I just can't consider myself a bad person

for putting a few pounds back on. Because I will put on and take off those pounds God only knows how many times in my life. That's the way life is.

Some of the guests I've talked with on *Good Morning America* over the years have also taught me a great deal about food and nutrition. I have found that cookbook authors have their own secrets about what works for them. After all, like a scientist in a lab, a cook learns what she knows by experimenting with new ideas.

I spoke again recently with some of my favorite food experts. Here are some of the tips they generously shared with me.

MARIE SIMMONS
(cookbook author):

Americans as a whole, I think, don't like the word "moderation." But really it's balance more than anything — eating everything, but in moderation. There's nothing *really* bad for you. It's the amounts you eat that are bad. If you love ice cream, for heaven's sake, have a bowl or half a bowl once a week. But don't eat it every night.

One way you can add a lot of flavor without adding a lot of calories and fat is with citrus. I use a lot of lemon and orange zest. There are volatile oils in the peel that give a wonderful flavor. Those oils mixed with herbs really make a nice combination. Some of my favorites are basil and orange, lemon and thyme, orange and basil with tomato, and rosemary with lemon and black pepper. Lime

juice is also just wonderful, on fish or in tomato salad or salsa. All these little duos or trios of flavors add so much. What you need to do is distract your palate from the flavor that is missing from all that extra fat.

Another thing I do a lot is make mixtures of chopped fruit and vegetables that I put on fish or serve with chicken. It's like a salsa, but I use mango or fresh peach with red onion, cilantro, and lime juice — and maybe throw some celery or cucumber in there.

I always have low-fat or nonfat plain yogurt in my refrigerator, and some kind of buttermilk. Despite its name, buttermilk is very low in fat. I like to mix strawberries (or peaches or bananas) with buttermilk and sugar in a blender. I freeze it, and it's like ice cream.

STEPHEN P. GULLO, PH.D.
(psychologist, author of Thin Tastes Better*):*

First of all, know your triggers. Most of the people who have come to me over the years were not heavy from food in general. They were heavy from a small number of foods or a small number of habits. The first thing I teach is, Know your "eating print": the types of foods you abuse, and the times of the day. This helps you to narrow your focus and not feel that it's you against the whole world of food.

For example, many women who work at home raising their children gain their weight between 3:00 and 6:00 in the afternoon: picking at food, eating standing up. And most of the men I've worked with have a problem of noshing when they turn on the TV. Super Bowl Sunday is also super-nosh Sunday.

The second tip is to understand control. Many of the people who have weight problems in America already know what to eat and what not to eat. However, they simply cannot do it, because they have control problems. People like Joan, who lose weight and keep it off, have identified their control problems.

More people fail on weight programs because of two reasons: cravings and deprivation. You need to understand what Joan understands: that food is not free, that you have to wear it. Our bodies have a budget. Treat calories like dollars. And ask yourself, Do I like it enough to wear it?

The other issue that trips people up is cravings. A craving is a feeling, not an irresistible force. The average food craving lasts from four to twelve minutes. And it's about planning, not willpower. Don't go without meals. If you go for longer than three to four hours without eating, your blood sugar gets low, and you start to think with your taste buds.

Just looking at foods that you have a great attraction to produces chemical changes in the brain: it turns on your appetite and starts a craving. Sin starts in the supermarket.

When you're going to be in a food situation, rehearse beforehand. Most people go into a restaurant, they sit in front of the bread basket, and all of a sudden, a wave comes over them: I have to have it. Rehearse in your mind ahead of time: "I'm going to see a bread basket. There

will be a dessert cart." When you see it, it won't hit you in the same magnetic, powerful way.

The most important concept in keeping in control with food is frequency. I talk about "boxing it in" or "boxing it out." You don't have to drop your favorite foods: you simply have to box them in if they're going to make you fat. If you can have that food just once a week, on special occasions, or when you go to a special restaurant — if you can "box it in" to then, that's fine. And if you can't do that and want to eat it and abuse it every day, then you have to learn to "box it out." If you cannot learn to have a little, it's far easier to learn to say no, thank you, than to do without ever tasting thinness.

There are many ways not to feel deprived. You want to remember that when you were eating that favorite food, your life was not a paradise. You were unhappy, were not able to wear the clothes you loved, and didn't have the look that you wanted. Most people forget that. As soon as they start to lose weight, they rewrite the script of their lives, thinking this food was some kind of magical treat that they're doing without.

The essence of long-term success in losing weight is not just changing your figure but also changing your head. If you're doing everything right but are walking around thinking, "I'm deprived. I can't wait to reward myself and treat myself," then you lose the weight but never lose the problem.

Sometimes eating is not about food. A number of the people who come to see me who are heavy don't even particularly like food. So many of us have learned, have been programmed by our society or our parents or grandparents, "Eat. You'll feel better."

In order to control overeating, you must give yourself alternative behaviors. Have a "911 person" in your life, so when you're under really severe stress, there's someone you can reach out to and talk to instead of reaching out to food. The other thing is exercise. It generates endorphins, which serve as antidepressants and anti-anxiety agents.

One other observation: people who eat under stress do not sit down to bake a cake or a lasagna. They reach for finger foods. They go around the house grabbing whatever they can find. If you're a stress eater, do not keep finger foods around.

If you have to keep snack foods around for your spouse and kids, go ahead — but don't buy your special favorites for them. Buy the small individual packs. And don't keep them out on the counter; remember, visual stimuli are the most powerful triggers.

Joan is living proof that you can lose weight and keep it off. Joan's success is also a reminder that there are millions of people who have learned to master food in their lives.

JULIA CHILD
(cookbook author, regular chef on Good Morning America for nine years):

Taking all the fat out of food is absolutely the wrong attitude. I think the correct one is that you have to change your mindset. Realize that you've been taking the wrong type of view about food.

Don't be as concerned about weight watching. Enjoy your food. Have a good time. The key is moderation and small helpings of a little bit of everything.

That upside-down triangle of having more fruits and vegetables, and less dairy and meat, works out very well. Use fresh food wherever possible, because in packaged food and frozen food, a lot of the flavor has gone out. Things have to taste good.

You must learn how to cook. You and a friend or your significant other can take one of these evening cooking classes, which are a great deal of fun. You don't have to be elaborate or a "gourmet" to do it well.

RUTH SPEAR
(journalist, author of Low Fat and Loving It):

Invest in an inexpensive calorie/fat guide. Keep a food diary for four to five days (which include a weekend) and write down the calories of what you ate and the fat grams that it contained. Then look at those things and say, "Well, these are the things that I am willing to eat less of." And that's different for everybody.

For example, I am not willing to give up 2 percent milk in my coffee, because I don't like the way it looks and tastes with skim milk. But I'm very willing to have ice cream only occasionally, and just have four or five mouthfuls. That's my tradeoff.

Maybe you're not willing to give up

meat. That's okay, but how about saying, "I'm only going to buy extra-lean hamburger." Or see if you can be happy with ground turkey instead.

Butter, margarine, and cooking oil have exactly the same amount of fat grams. I don't use margarine, because while margarine doesn't have the kind of saturated fat that butter does, it has transfatty acids, which are also unhealthy.

You can make low-fat meals flavorful by following certain general planning rules. Select cooking methods such as broiling, baking, poaching, steaming, and braising instead of frying or sautéing. Use nonstick pans so that you don't have to use a lot of fat. Start onions and garlic in a tablespoon of olive oil and then add broth or water so that they can steam-sauté.

There's no question that fat is a conveyor of flavor. Make up for lowered fat by using a lot of herbs and spices. Fat also has a "mouth feel" that satisfies us. But when you cut down on fat, your mouth gets unused to the feel of fat — to such a point that when you do eat fatty things, they taste and feel rather revolting, sort of slimy.

Develop an eating plan by taking a quick look at the USDA food pyramid and understanding that grains, fruits, and vegetables should be about 65 percent of what you eat. That can be in any format you like.

It might be grain casseroles. We eat risottos, and bulgur wheat pilaf made with raisins and pine nuts, then cooked in low-sodium chicken broth. They're so delicious that sometimes I have to remind myself to eat whatever else is on my plate.

Explore vegetables that you don't now eat. By oven-roasting vegetables, you can make really rather ordinary things taste absolutely delicious with the addition of very little oil. By cooking at high heat, the natural sugars that are present in many vegetables, such as carrots or sweet potatoes, caramelize slightly. And you get something that is so delicious you may actually find yourself craving it.

Another thing you can do is make a list of the things that you and your family eat frequently. Put the fattiest ones — for example, spare ribs — at the top of the list, and go on down to the least fatty ones. That way, you identify the ones that can only be an occasional treat, and you can start reshaping your repertoire.

When you're shopping, go right to the vegetable department and look for the loveliest things you can find. Build up a repertoire of nice, tasty ways to cook vegetables as a centerpiece. Think of meat and chicken as demoted in your mind to a flavoring.

You can also plan two or three meatless meals a week: a lentil chili or a pasta with baked eggplant in a savory tomato sauce. You will find ones that are utterly satisfying for you, so that you don't miss meat.

Don't eat eggs more than two or three times a week, and poach or boil rather than fry them. You can even scramble them in the microwave: put one in a measuring cup with a tablespoon of water, microwave it on high for 30 seconds, then stir it lightly with a fork, and microwave it for another 20. And you'll have a lovely, fluffy egg, with no added fat.

Avoid Southern-fried chicken, Wiener schnitzel, or anything else that's breaded and fried. If you do have to eat it, just remove the breading. Skip anything that's already made up in a buttery sauce, like béarnaise or hollandaise.

For snacks, try graham crackers, flatbread crackers, breadsticks, or matzo. Try some air-popped popcorn with a glass of tomato or V-8 juice. Keep favorite berries and squares of melon already speared on toothpicks in the fridge. Nonfat tortilla chips, which you can dip in salsa, are a great snack.

For dessert, make fruit cobblers and crisps instead of a two-crust pie. Another pie ploy is a graham cracker crust, which uses only two tablespoons of melted butter or margarine. Angel food cake has virtually no fat. You can serve it with your favorite berries for dessert.

STEVEN RAICHLEN
(author of the award-winning High-Flavor, Low-Fat Cookbook *series):*

The most important point I want to make is to use flavor instead of fat to make foods taste delicious. That's the whole key. One technique is using vegetable stock or chicken stock in place of heavy cream, oil, or butter in a myriad of dishes — for example, my spaghetti with white bean sauce (see page 133). You take away fat but you keep the flavor.

Fruit purees are great for baking. You can use prune puree instead of butter in chocolate cakes and brownies. You can use applesauce instead of shortening in oatmeal cookies. In my baked stuffed apples, I use grated banana instead of butter for the stuffing, so you get that kind of moist, luscious mouth feel, but without the fat.

One great thing to use for a creamy texture in foods is the new nonfat sour cream. Unlike regular sour cream, it doesn't curdle when you boil it. It also thickens, so that you can actually make a cream sauce with it.

Fresh herbs also add flavor without adding fat. One of my favorite secrets is lemon zest: the grated outer peel has a very vibrant, almost electric lemon flavor, without the sourness.

I think Joan looks like a million bucks, so she must be doing something right.

SHARON TYLER HERBST
(food writer, author of The Food Lover's Tiptionary*):*

The thing we want to do is make the mouth happy, but we don't have to have those high-caloric things. In sauces and soups, I suggest using nonfat or low-fat evaporated milk because it adds a wonderful texture without the extra calories of cream.

You can create a low-fat salad dressing using half a cup of nonfat yogurt and a cup of fresh herbs, such as basil or parsley. Or add a little garlic and a tablespoon of lemon juice and put it in the blender. You absolutely don't need oil in marinades. Instead, add wine, or V-8 or tomato juice.

An occasional hamburger can be a comfort food. A neat way to prepare one is to buy lean ground beef or other meat and substitute shredded potatoes or carrots or cooked, mashed pinto beans for a third or half of the meat.

EVELYN TRIBOLE
(co-author of Intuitive Eating):

Making progress is what matters. One meal, one snack, one day is not going to make or break you. You must make peace with food. If you truly want to eat something, it's okay. Otherwise, deprivation will kill you.

If you really believe you can't have a particular food, by the time you do have it, you end up overeating it. Because eating becomes like "the last supper": this is the last chance you're ever going to have it again, so you'd better get it now while you can.

From a weight-loss standpoint and from a health standpoint, you've got to feed your body and to honor your hunger. There are people who are running around with not enough food in their bodies. They end up overeating. When you're ravenous, you don't care — you grab anything.

Always look for ways to cut the fat where you're not going to miss it. For example, when you're making a cake or a casserole, you can usually substitute egg whites for eggs. And for each yolk you get rid of, you're removing 213 milligrams of cholesterol from your diet and from the mouths of your loved ones.

A lot of marinades call for oil. Instead, you can use a combination of chicken broth and fruit juice. For every half a cup, you'll again save about 900 calories.

You need to keep some of your favorites, but it's a matter of using less. If something calls for a cup of walnuts, you could use half that amount. And you're still saving almost 400 calories and about 40 grams of fat. The same thing goes for chocolate chips in cookies.

When you're shopping for foods, choose ones that have no more than three grams of fat per 100 calories. You also need to look at serving sizes — not what it says on the label, but how much you actually eat. If you end up eating a whole bag of fat-free chips, that's going to be 800 calories, as opposed to the 100 calories in a "serving."

Chicken thighs, even without the skin, can have more fat than some cuts of beef. It's better to choose chicken breast — that's the lowest in fat. Pork tenderloin is actually a very low-fat cut of meat.

There's this big trend right now to think of carbohydrates as fattening — and they're not. We actually need a minimum of six grain servings a day: breads, pastas, and rice.

Potatoes aren't fattening by themselves. It would take about sixteen potatoes to make a pound of fat! And pasta's a fabulous food. But pasta, like any food if you eat too much of it, can make you fat. If you go into a restaurant and clean your plate, you're probably eating too much food, whether it's pasta or something else.

There are some people now who are so

into fat-free eating that they eat no grams of fat. They are truly fatphobic. They forget that we actually need fat in every cell of our body, for a lot of vital functions. It's important to stress that we need some fat in our diets.

It comes down to two things: how much and the quality of what you're eating.

Now that we've heard from the experts, I'll offer my two bits of advice. These are the basic rules I follow in my everyday life:

- We're all human and we will make mistakes.
- You will fall off from time to time.
- You will gain five to ten pounds.
- Don't panic!
- Don't beat yourself up.
- Don't buy bigger clothes . . . lose the weight!
- Learn you don't have to be perfect.

At some point you have to be happy with the weight you've achieved. And it may not match your idea of perfection. I am not my vision of "Miss Perfect" and never will be. That's just the way it is, and I'm over it. You can make yourself way too crazy.

I'm too busy doing other things to devote my whole life to staying at a certain weight. Would I like to be five pounds thinner? Sure, it would be great. But the fact is that I'm not willing to make those trade-offs. Three kids later, I'm pretty happy where I am, thank you. I may not wear the smallest bikini on the beach, but I'm wearing one.

Chapter 4

OH, WHAT A RELIEF IT IS . . . FIT FEELS GOOD

How does fit feel? I have said on numerous occasions over the past few years that I feel so great and have so much energy, I almost don't know what to do with myself. I almost feel guilty, as though I might have someone else's share.

Physical fitness is a little strange for me, because I grew up being the antithesis of physical. I was always the teenager who would write fake notes to get out of gym class. Not only did I stay away from school sports, but I wouldn't even try out for cheerleading — it just seemed like way too much jumping around for me!

Experts say that about 5 percent of Americans are born to be thin. They can eat almost anything and will still be slender. But for the remaining 95 percent of us, particularly as we get older, to be thin and stay thin requires learning how to adjust to the changes in our bodies. This means altering our eating habits and stepping up our activity level.

In our teens and twenties, we burn up many more calories than we do in our thirties, forties, or fifties. As a matter of fact, for each decade that we age, we burn approxi-mately 750 fewer calories per week. Now I understand the expression "Those who can adapt endure, and those who cannot adapt perish." Being thin and staying thin as the years go by is a process of continuing adaptation. To age well is not an accident.

Throughout this book I emphasize that the combination of understanding nutrition, making the right food choices, and exercising regularly has been the key to my success. In this chapter, I share what I've learned about starting and sticking to an effective exercise program.

Get the Green Light from Your Doctor

Before you start an exercise program, it's important to get a medical checkup. This can help you avoid aggravating any existing medical conditions, such as heart disease, high blood pressure, and back problems. Hearing a doctor tell you how exercise reduces your risk of disease can also be very motivating! I know it was for me. I was scared to death that the extra weight I was carrying around would increase my susceptibility to some major illness as well as injury.

My exercise video, Workout America

Get Some Support and Guidance

Try to get someone to exercise with you, to be your workout buddy. Because of my crazy schedule, it was hard for me to commit myself to a specific time that fit in with any of my friends' normal daytime work schedules. So I hired a fitness trainer to serve the same purpose: to keep me motivated.

My trainer, Barbara Brandt, also taught me the right way to exercise. When I first did sit-ups, she said, "You're just expending energy. You're not doing anything to help your body." Half-remembered high school calisthenics won't cut it; you need a model to follow.

If you'd like to try working with a trainer, most gyms these days have someone on staff or can make a referral. You can hire someone one-on-one for just a few sessions to teach

you exercises that meet your needs. Another way to get started is to join an exercise class led by a trainer.

What should you look for in a trainer? Personal fitness trainers are not legally required to have any special training or credentials. However, there are widely known groups that certify trainers, such as the American College of Sports Medicine (ACSM), the National Strength and Conditioning Association (NSCA), the American Council on Exercise (ACE), and the American Fitness Aerobic Association (AFAA). Many gyms insist on this kind of certification for their trainers.

You can ask whether the trainer has a college degree (preferably a master's) in exercise physiology, sports medicine, dance, physical education, or something similar. A good trainer should also ask about your health and exercise history, and what your goals are. Finally, the trainer shouldn't ask you to do anything that really hurts. If you feel something isn't right, get another opinion.

You can also get a good exercise video to follow at home. The tape serves as your own convenient personal trainer and workout buddy. I released my own fitness video, *Workout America,* so that I could share my trainer's expertise. Barbara leads the class on the video, which offers a two-part, well-rounded program. Part one is a dance aerobic workout, and part two is a muscle-toning/flexibility workout that focuses on specific body parts.

The important thing to remember when picking a video is that it should offer a safe

Barbara Brandt (front, right) leading my exercise video

and repeatable workout from a fitness professional. If you don't learn how to do exercises properly, you're wasting your time. You're sweating, but you're not toning and are risking injury.

A good trainer or video can help you in ways you may not even have considered. When I started working with Barbara, she said, "I know you're here to lose weight, but I'd like to do a *lot* more with you. For example, I would like to help you improve your posture. When you sit on your show, you let the top of your body sink down into the bottom part of your body. It makes your shoulders come forward, and you don't present as well as you could. Tighten your abs and lengthen your torso, and see how much better you'll look and feel."

Today, one of the comments I hear most often from co-hosts who fill in when Charlie's away is that I sit up so straight, they feel like they look short sitting next to me. In fact, I'll let you in on a little secret: some of

them put a wooden board beneath their cushion of the *Good Morning America* sofa, to keep them sitting up straighter and at the same height as I am during the show!

Cover All the Bases

According to Judy Gantz, M.A., CMA, a professor of dance and kinesiology at the University of California, Los Angeles, a well-rounded program should focus on four areas. First, there's aerobic exercises: ones that work your heart and lungs. These also do the best job of burning fat. Brisk walking, swimming, bike riding, and aerobic dance all fall into this group. For best results, you need to do this kind of exercise for twenty to forty minutes, three to five days a week. If you're exercising at a healthy pace, you should be able to chat with your buddy but still feel that you're exerting yourself.

The treadmill was my number-one way to burn off calories. It also helped build my endurance and tone my legs. One nice thing about the treadmill is that it's easy to learn, and I could use it on my own right away.

The second area to cover is muscle-strength training, which helps tone, burn calories, and improve posture. These exercises work by repeatedly using a source of resistance, such as gravity or your own body weight. You generally do each exercise eight to ten times (called a "set"), for two or three sets. Your goal is to do exercises that work each of the major muscle groups, starting with the large muscles in the hips, butt, thighs, trunk, and shoulders.

For me, I really needed to work with my trainer, Barbara, to learn how to do these toning exercises. I needed not only to see how she did the exercises but to get to know my own muscles. That way, I could tell if I was doing the exercises right, as well as track my own progress.

Try not to get discouraged as you start doing these exercises. It takes a while to learn how to identify and call into action specific muscle groups. I know that when I first started, I felt like a total dork. I just couldn't seem to zero in on my muscles, let alone control their function.

The third important area is flexibility training, which keeps your muscles relaxed and supple. Stretching areas like your neck, torso, back, shoulders, chest, hips, and calves three or more times a week not only feels great and reduces stiffness but also increases your range of motion. It's important not to

strain or bounce when you stretch. Try to hold each position for ten to sixty seconds.

The fourth area of focus for your exercise plan is coordination and posture. As I found, your posture — the way you sit, how you walk — tells people a lot about the shape you're in and how you feel about yourself. Any new skill that involves rhythm, timing, and balance — aerobic dance, tennis, and so on — helps your coordination and posture. It's the foundation for healthy joints and muscles.

Slow and Steady Does the Job

BARBARA BRANDT:
Some people tend to approach working out the same way as the "weekend warrior" athlete does: they get an entire week's worth of exercise in a weekend. It takes time to put a lot of weight on, and it should be understood that it takes a certain amount of time to take weight off.

Find out how you can build exercise into your schedule on a consistent basis — not where you're doing so many hours one week, and then nothing the next.

Most experts say people should not really lose more than a pound and a half — two pounds tops — per week. If you take off too much weight quickly, you lose lean muscle mass instead of losing fat. You're also more likely to regain the weight, because you're setting an impossible pace.

Set a Series of Small Goals

Start with some short-term, "bite-sized" goals, rather than focusing on your long-term, big objective. If you have reasonable and attainable goals — a five-pound weight loss for the month, an increase in the amount of weight you can lift by so much — you won't feel overwhelmed and defeated. With small goals, each little success adds to a pattern and an expectation of more successes.

I learned to set small goals for both weight loss and endurance. When I first got on the treadmill, I was dead meat after fifteen minutes. Now, I could do an hour and a half if I wanted to. Sometimes I have to make myself get *off* the treadmill, because I know I'm going to do myself in. To this day, to keep myself on track, I'm constantly setting goals for myself. I always give myself a situation in the not-too-distant future for which I want to look my best: a photo shoot, a special date, or fitting into a particular dress for a party.

Expect Some Frustration at First

In the beginning, exercise is not much fun. Why? Because you're moving ignored-for-God-knows-how-long muscles that can't get the job done. It's going to take some time to find and identify your muscles, use them a little bit, and gain some strength. It also takes shedding some of those pounds: it's a lot easier to lift 130 pounds than it is to lift 160. So you have to have some stick-to-itiveness and hang in there.

My trainer encouraged me to look at exercise like a sport. You're trying to hit that tennis ball and keep missing it. You're learning how to ski and keep falling down. It's the same way with exercise. It's no fun just snow-plowing and falling down on the ski slope. Tennis is not much fun until you can have a rally. But say to yourself, "Wow, this is going to be really fun once I learn how to do it." That helped me look at exercise in a positive way, instead of seeing it as a big, fat drag.

Always Warm Up and Cool Down

One of the things Barbara really had to drum into me was the importance of stretching before and after workouts. When I would work out on my own without her, I was my own worst enemy — practically an accident waiting to happen. God forbid I should actually spend time in the gym doing something that didn't burn calories!

I now use stretching before the show every morning. It loosens me up and really wakes me up before I go on the air. Finally, whenever I feel achy or really stressed out, I have found that taking five minutes just to stretch my neck, shoulders, and back is really soothing. It can work wonders on a headache, especially if it is muscle-related.

BARBARA BRANDT:
I had to teach Joan the importance of warming up her muscles. Generally speaking, people who are very weight conscious don't value a warm-up, don't

value a cooldown, and don't value stretching, because these activities don't burn calories. And Joan epitomized the person who just wanted to see the weight come off. It didn't matter what it took or at what cost, or if she hurt her hamstring a little bit — that was okay as long as she was down a pound.

Injuring yourself defeats the whole purpose, and it takes you out of commission. If you have to attend to a sprained ankle or a pulled hamstring, then you can't be on the treadmill.

I joke that I needed to work with Joan to protect her against herself. I found she would get on the treadmill and just beat up her body. While the machine can be used constructively, it can also be used irresponsibly. If you just get on, and haven't stretched out and don't cool down, then there's a real likelihood that you might hurt a muscle, which is what she tended to do at first.

Use Exercise (Not Food)
for Stress Relief

When I started working out, I was thinking about looking better and about future health risks. I didn't realize exercise could also do much more for me. For one thing, being fit made me much more able to focus mentally, to think more clearly. I think I became much better at work.

Exercise also allowed me to let go of a whole lot of stress and anger. I used to let a lot of little things bother me. My former assistant, Debbie Bergenfeld, once told her successor, Samantha Berg, "You work for a different person than I worked for. If things had happened during the day that happen now, she would have been all upset and angry, maybe even in tears."

I am a highly scheduled individual — to the point that some people would consider obsessive. But I have to do so much that if I didn't schedule myself, I'd be running around like a chicken with its head cut off. I'd never be able to do everything I need to do, and I'd be harried and hassled. Consequently, I can practically tell you what I'm going to be doing on a Tuesday four months from now.

But it used to be that if somebody put a dent in my armor and threw off my schedule, it would upset me — and, usually, I'd eat. That was my form of coping. Eating always made me feel better.

That's not to say I never get upset or unhappy anymore. I'm a normal human being! But now I'm more inclined to go home and put on my workout clothes. Just recently, I had a frazzled day, getting home at 8:30 at night. And I was thinking, "I'd really like to just go and find something good to eat in the refrigerator."

Then I told myself, "Wait a minute! Why am I going to let someone hassling me force me to do something that's bad for me? I won't let that happen to me! Instead, I'm going downstairs to my little gym and work out — do something that's good for me. And when I walk back upstairs, I'll feel good about myself."

Can you see the grin on my face? It's how I look every time I jump my horse.

At home, I can use my treadmill or my free weights, do some isometrics, or use my exercise video. And when I do an hour on the treadmill, I totally forget everything. I approach stress from a completely different viewpoint now. But it did not happen overnight.

Stick with the Program, But Don't Beat Yourself Up

I've found that the longer I go without exercising, the harder it is to start again. So I try

not to let that happen. But you know something? There are times when it does, because I can't help it. For example, when I'm in Europe for two weeks with *Good Morning America,* and we fly from country to country to country, I may say, "As soon as we get there, I'm going to work out!"

Well, there's no time! After the show, there's a production meeting, I have to read the scripts and the research, and I'm lucky if I can write out some notes and get into bed by 10:00 — so I can get up earlier the next morning and start again! And I can't kick myself around the block five times for not getting to the hotel gym, which probably closed before I even arrived.

So there are times when I can't exercise. But I know it's happened before, and I can get up to speed again. But I used to *panic.* And fear is disabling. Researchers have even found that fear suppresses your immune system. Fear and panic get in the way of positive, constructive decision making.

Find a Sport or Activity You Love

Looking good and feeling good are only part of what I get from my exercise program. To me, the really amazing part of my transformation is how truly *physical* my life has become. I stopped being a spectator and started being a participant.

We're supposed to be a nation of fitness junkies. Everywhere you look, there are constant reminders of what a perky country we are. Nike commercials tell us to "just do it,"

With my oldest daughter, Jamie, after a winning day at the horse show

Reebok has named our planet, even Diet Coke portrays a fit image. But in exercise, there's a broad gap between our public image and our private reality.

According to a February 1995 report in the *Journal of the American Medical Association,* only 22 percent of Americans engage in moderate physical activity. It defines moderate physical activity as the equivalent of brisk walking for about thirty minutes almost daily. One out of four of us admits to doing no exercise at all. Given these statistics, it should be no surprise that we are a fatter nation than we ever have been. Even though our caloric intake has dropped by 2 percent, overall, 34 percent of the population in the United States is considered overweight. That's up 8 percent since 1980.

I was always well intentioned when planning to exercise but could always find an excuse for bailing out. I used to sign up for so many lessons, there weren't enough hours in the day to participate in all of them. Of course, I wanted to be great at everything I tried: tennis, racquetball, horseback riding, even rock climbing.

I found out quickly that if you spread yourself too thin (no pun intended), you'll never be great at any one particular thing. So I realized that once again, I had to make a choice. I needed to find a sport that would keep my attention — and would help motivate me to maintain my regular exercise routine. Since my daughter Jamie rides, I chose horseback riding. I am extremely glad that I did, as it has become an integral part of our family life. You can bet that nine times out of ten, when I'm off *Good Morning America,* I am on a horse somewhere.

My particular event is called Adult Amateur Hunters. I always get a kick out of this competition because we're all working people who jump our horses over three-foot fences as though they were nine-foot walls. It's hard to describe the feeling I get when I'm riding and competing, but a dead giveaway is the ear-to-ear smile on my face as I leave the ring. I wish all people could find something that they love as much as I love riding and discover that feeling.

This desire and ability to participate in life, to challenge yourself, and to feel so vibrant and alive, is a whole dimension hardly considered when you first start to "get into shape." It's not just about pounds anymore, it's about how good fitness feels. What a huge relief it is to protect your health instead of destroying it. To just breathe easier . . . to have better-looking skin . . . standing, walking, running, jumping, even just getting out of your chair with ease and grace. It's about feeling energized during the day and sleeping better at night. It's about being able to think more clearly and perform better. It's about being a lot less cranky and a lot more peaceful. It's about standing tall and presenting yourself with pride. These are wonderful gifts to give yourself.

Chapter 5

LOOKING INWARD

Some years ago I interviewed Farrah Fawcett and commented on her natural healthy beauty. She seemed so vibrant. I remember she attributed it to her joie de vivre. At the time, I wasn't really sure what that meant. After the interview, I looked it up, and found that it means "a love of life." That phrase has always stuck with me. Only now do I really understand what it means.

True fitness is far more than losing unwanted pounds. It's as much about your emotional and mental fitness as it is your physical fitness. You are in control of all of these. Once you've taken the steps and have dealt with the outside, the natural next step is to look inward. There have been numerous articles written on this subject, and it seems that nearly all people who go through a physical transformation of their body — shedding the top layers — eventually look below the surface. To realize your ultimate dream of total fitness and well-being, you have to be willing to leave that comfort zone you've created for yourself and take risks in order to change and grow.

As I delved inside myself, I questioned whether it was my own self-doubt and fear of what might be on the other side that was holding me back. Having unsuccessfully attempted to change my life and improve my health too many times in the past, why would I now suddenly find success? Worse yet, was I just setting myself up to once again fail miserably?

The answers to these questions are not cut-and-dried. It has only been through the catharsis of writing this book that I have come up with some reasonable explanations. It's been amazingly therapeutic and helpful for me to probe this area of my life. Everyone has their personal dilemmas, and sometimes it's just easier to ignore them. When they weigh your life down enough that you no longer can ignore them, you have to face what's staring back at you in the mirror. For most of us, myself included, that's a lot easier said than done.

My career was pretty much where I wanted it to be. I host the number-one morning show in America, and have done so for nearly twenty years. I've always had a slew of outside projects that were at the very least keeping me busy. The difficulty came in the outside projects that were being created for me by someone else. My time was not my own, and I really did not say or do a thing about it. I was literally working myself into oblivion. While I wasn't unhappy and I am quite grateful that I was a part of many successful professional undertakings, all of which offered helpful information to so many people, it was the lack of ability to make these decisions for myself that became harder and harder to take. I began to feel that there was a real lack of control in every aspect of my life.

I'm partly at fault for allowing this to happen. Perhaps part of me liked being taken care of in that way. In looking back, I wish that I'd had the self-confidence then that I do today to have made these decisions for myself. I now recognize that this shortage of confidence and control created a major barrier for me all of those years.

❖

It was definitely my own fears that held me back. Discovering what those were and taking them on, one by one, was part of the process in my journey to fitness. The changes I made affected many crucial elements in my life. I knew that I was unhappy and very discontented with my marriage, but being out there again as a single woman frightened me even more. There was a certain comfort that I had gotten used to. And like most of us, I was not sure that I had what it took inside of me to give up that security, albeit a false one. My discomfort, however, screamed so loudly inside my head that I had to shut it out in order to get a grip and make the toughest decision of my life. I call it my leap of faith. Was I willing to jump headfirst, and do whatever it took to make my life a better one?

A lot of you might recall the day that *Good Morning America* aired my bungee jump off a bridge while on location in Queenstown, New Zealand. The symbolism of that remarkable and most definitely memorable experience is quite fascinating. As I stood on the edge of that bridge, 150 feet above the river, I slowly inched my way out to my jump position. All I had was a rope tied around my ankles, and I was to dive toward the water. From my perspective, the man who was to retrieve me and release me from my bungee cord was so far away that he looked like an ant.

I dug right down to the bottom of my soul and found the courage and the will to take that dive. I had to trust that it was going to be all right. I had to believe in myself. With a deep breath and a little prayer, I dove, like a swan, arms out and eyes wide open. With every passing second I came closer to the water. As if by magic, I rebounded without ever touching the cold blue river that day. As I made my way to the boat, I felt exhilarated at what I had just experienced. And I also realized something very important, perhaps for the first time in my life: I had the courage, the strength, and the ability to do whatever it is that I set my mind to.

After my jump that day, I went crazy with excitement and wrote everyone I knew about this incredible experience. I realized this wasn't the first time I had taken a flying leap into unknown territory, requiring my personal strength and courage to know that somehow it would be all right. If pressed on

Taking my "leap of faith," bungee jumping in New Zealand

which was scarier, "finding myself" or jumping off that bridge, I'm not sure I could make a choice. Obviously, the bungee jump was symbolic of the previous years I had gone through. Quite frankly, there was a moment on that bridge when I wasn't certain I could actually go through with it. But I was so mad for even doubting myself. This time, I wasn't going to let my fear hold me back.

After my jump, as I sat there on the edge of the river, I knew that I had passed into the next phase of my journey. Somehow, I knew that this phase held unlimited potential. If I could bungee jump in New Zealand or ice-climb in Alaska, surely I could face any challenge. But I needed to take that final leap of faith.

Now, I'm not suggesting that you leap off a bridge in order to deal with your issues. What I hope you get from this story is that you can do anything you set your mind to. You can lose that last ten pounds. You can get that promotion at work. You can find happiness right there, inside of you. You can't wait for good things to happen to you; you have to make them happen. You have to stop weighing every option, fearing failure, and get up off your butt and just do it.

Start by setting goals for yourself. Set small goals at first, so that you can experience positive results and achieve them in the short term. Nothing motivates me more than achieving a goal that I have set for myself, no matter what the size. If you want to be some-

Some of my adventures over the past few years have included ice-climbing in Alaska, parakiting in New Zealand, and white-water rafting.

one who fulfills your dreams, you have to stop talking about them and live them. Without action, there is no change; and without change, there is no growth. Change affects growth, and you are in complete control of both. You can't sit around waiting for the planets to be aligned or to suddenly feel more confident or to just be in the mood to get started. The fastest way I know to make things happen is just to dive in headfirst.

You'd think I would have known this by now, since my mom always tried to instill in me as a kid that "impossible" does not exist in our vocabulary. She worked hard to give me a "there's nothing I can't do" attitude. It resulted in a real survivor mentality. I have never viewed myself as a victim. This attitude has always been extremely important in my ability to achieve positive results.

At some point you have to decide that you believe you can do it and that you're committed to the fact that it's really important. There's a certain leap of faith that you just have to take.

And interestingly, what that decision does in the end is give you the ability to take more leaps of faith, to try other things. You need to get some successes under your belt to know you can do them. And I think a lot of people, especially women, really sell themselves short. They think they can do only so much in life. But really, they could do so much more, be so much more.

When you get happy with yourself, when you feel fit and healthy, you walk into a room a different person. People react to you in a different way. Your life changes. When you

finally zip open your cocoon and emerge at the other end of that metamorphosis, what's so amazing is that your life has changed; you are a renewed person. And your array of options from which to choose is so much more fun and exciting.

What you think you can do and accomplish in life totally changes. I go into things these days, whether they're business projects or social situations, that five years ago I don't think I would have been able to handle. I've done things that I never thought I could do — saying, "I can do this," even if I had no prior experience.

When I was asked to do an exercise video, my first thoughts were, "I can't do this! Are they out of their minds? How can they offer this to me?" Then I said to myself, "Why not? I can do it." The best part about it was that now I had a new goal: to be in peak condition by taping day. Because if I was going to shoot an exercise video, I needed to be in the best physical shape I'd ever been in. I was going to have to dance and do aerobics and floor exercises over and over, for an entire day.

Not only did I do it, but I must tell you what a kick it is to have people walk up to me and say, "I got your video a couple of months ago, and I'm doing it all the time now. My stomach's really getting flat!" I hear comments like this practically every day. Knowing that I'm having a positive effect on other people's lives makes all the hard work worthwhile.

❖

You know the old saying, Don't wish for something too hard, you just might get it?

Giving the "thumbs up" after landing an F-18 on the deck of the USS Eisenhower

For years, I fought to have prime-time specials as part of my contract with ABC. I wanted to expand my career into nighttime programming. Well, I won the battle and now had to face the war. It was a war between my desire to do new things and my fear that I couldn't.

I had asked for prime-time specials, which required me to take on physically challenging activities in front of a camera. Would I be able to deliver? Once again I faced unknown territory, producing and appearing in my "Behind Closed Doors" specials on ABC. And once again, I persevered and found that I would take on this new challenge the only way I knew how, by just diving in headfirst.

Five years ago, these specials would not have been a reality, because physically I would not have been able to do them. And now, in a way, they epitomize my new being. The idea of "Behind Closed Doors" is that I take you, vicariously, to places where you otherwise couldn't go, and do things that you'd otherwise never get to do. ABC teamed me with two of the best adventure producers in the business, Eric Schotz and Bill Paolantonio. From the outset, they believed in my ability to do these specials 100 percent. It took me time, but their confidence in me helped instill my own.

For one of the segments, I flew in an F-18 jet and landed on the USS *Eisenhower* aircraft carrier. In order to do this, though, I had to pass an incredibly rigorous navy survival test. The parachute drop. The ejection simulator. The high-altitude chamber where you experience a lack of oxygen, causing you to lose motor skills and, for some, consciousness. Not to mention the swimming test, which included being submerged and turned upside down in a mock aircraft to see if you could escape and make your way to the surface. And I always thought pools were just for lying around in the sun!

Going through naval training for my F-18 flight

This adventure-seeking became like an aphrodisiac for me. The more I challenged myself, the more I wanted to push myself. Each segment became a test in which I had to push the envelope. So next I chose an adventure on a submarine with the Navy Seals . . . one I will never forget.

This time, I had to pass another series of grueling tests. (What is it about me and the navy, anyway?) First, it was fire training at the submarine training school. I had to don so much gear, I practically passed out from the weight of it. The worst was yet to come. We "Baby Seals" had to fight a gas-controlled, raging fire in the engine room and learn how to put it out. Let me tell you, *that* melted my mascara!

Then, to ensure that all of the makeup on my face was completely removed, they sent me into a leak simulator. The room looked like the inside of a submarine, but every few minutes they would let go with these intense water sprays, at 150 pounds of pressure. In fact, I got shot in the face once, and it gave me blurred vision for three days! They teach you to get control of the leak, by pressing a piece of metal around it and screwing on a metal clamp to secure it. But as fast as you get one done, they spring another one on you. And in case you're wondering, it's not bath water that they shoot at you. It's so cold it makes your teeth chatter.

They saved the most daunting task for last. They fill a room with water. Then you must hold your breath and swim down through an escape route to safety. But all the training paid off when we surfaced off the coast of Puerto Rico under moonlit skies in a U.S. Navy nuclear submarine. Within minutes, I was deployed out of a top hatch with a

With the Navy Seals. Guess which one is me. . . .

dozen highly trained Navy Seals. Before the night was over, we would take a beach on a small U.S. Naval training island, with live gunfire.

Five years ago, if someone had told me I would be doing this stuff, I would have said, "Yeah, right! I'm sure going to do that!" Being able to take part in once-in-a-lifetime adventures like these is one of the greatest rewards for taking my journey to fitness.

❖

Now that I have completely beaten you over the head with the idea of taking action, it's equally important to learn how to slow down and take some time out for yourself. Believe

it or not, learning how to relax and take the time to stop and smell the roses was probably the most difficult part of my journey.

When was the last time you let up on the pedal long enough to stop punishing yourself with self-imposed pressures? You know the ones I'm talking about: to stick to your diet, be more consistent with your workouts, get into the tighter jeans, build more muscle, be more successful . . . the list goes on. And it's you who makes that list! Well, how about giving yourself a break?

No one can put as much pressure on us as we put on ourselves. And it's good to a point. But not if you push yourself past the point of diminishing returns into anxiety, negativity, and guilt. I know, because I'm guilty. But if you're not careful, these self-imposed pressures can really sap your energy. And they can eat away at your sense of self-worth and accomplishment. All too often frustration and anger set in . . . and this is when we give up and throw in the towel.

This vicious cycle affects your immune system, your recuperative powers, and your emotional well-being. So you must stop every now and then and let up on yourself. I found that there were times I was spending more time thinking about what I should be doing than actually doing it. We put way too many demands on ourselves and then find that we can't possibly live up to those expectations. It's a definite recipe for disaster. You need to stop and take a breath! I chose meditation to help me find that "zone." Whatever you decide to do, you have to learn how to give yourself a break.

It's not easy, I know. I used to think that any "down time" was wasted time, which, of course, just increased my feelings of anxiety and guilt. Only in the last year have I been able to truly break out of this cycle. I feel so much better now — enjoying my breaks, luxuriating in "my time," so that I come back to my tasks much stronger and happier.

I once heard someone compare this to a child reaching for a toy on a shelf . . . stretching and trying so hard to reach that shelf. When she couldn't reach it, she got frustrated and gave up and cried, even though her goal was only a few inches away. She didn't realize

that sometimes you have to stop and take a moment, take a deep breath, and bend your knees to gather your strength so that you can make that final leap to success. I've always loved that analogy.

Sometimes we need to be reminded that there really is a value to taking a step back, clearing your head, and maybe just simply relaxing, so that we can come back to the task much more focused, much more energized, and better able to accomplish what we set out to do. We need to accept that down time, relaxation, and fun are other important elements to ensure a successful program for achieving a state of total well-being.

Pick something you enjoy for your down time — a massage, meditation, a bath with candles and no phones, a tennis game, lunch with your friends with no appointment to rush to . . . get the picture? As someone whose life has always been totally scheduled, this has been a hard lesson for me to learn. But I've finally come to understand the value of relaxing!

❖

Understanding the value and the power of visualization was an even more foreign concept to me than relaxing. Visualization is a technique I learned from Dr. Sam Schwartz in which you close your eyes and picture something happening in living color. Experts say that the mind thinks in pictures and that 70 percent of what you see and perceive in your mind you can actually achieve.

When I first heard about visualization, I thought that it was a total crock. I had gone to see Sam Schwartz for some nutritional counseling to help me get over a weight-loss plateau. After I left his office, I sat in my car taking a moment to look at the plethora of written information he had given me. I came across a page titled "Writing Your Own Script." Amidst all of the nutritional handouts, that little rascal had slipped in a one-page recommendation on the benefits of visualization.

As I read through each paragraph, I could literally hear the theme from the *Twilight Zone.* What kind of kook was this guy? He wanted me to steal away a few minutes every four hours or so, and focus on my self-image? Like I had a few minutes every four hours to give! What did any of this have to do with what I was supposed to be eating? This one-page dissertation said that if I wanted to be at a lesser weight, I must be able to see myself that way. I was to visualize my figure; see my fit, trim body clearly in my mind; and then go after that image. It said, "You are what you see — not what you eat. Believe it and make it happen."

The paper stressed that this mental exercise was just as important as my physical exercise. It concluded that "you must be able to see yourself the way you want to be. Then guide your body in that direction. Follow that image. It will lead you where you want to be. You are in control." Could this really help, to just think about how I wanted to look and feel? I simply did not get the mind-body connection yet.

It would be some time later that I would learn what Sam really wanted me to do was to see myself at the end of this road I was headed down. Just as an architect cannot design a house without a complete vision of what that house is going to look like when it's finished, you can't begin to change until you know where you're headed. What he was telling me was that I could write my own script, ending it any way I wanted to.

I can tell you that I have used visualization to help me deal with a lot of moments in my life. When I am preparing to compete in a horse show, I close my eyes and actually go through the course as if I'm really riding it on my horse. I feel the jumps, sense my timing, and become better prepared to compete during my round.

In order to see myself as a thinner person, I had to visualize myself as a thinner person. I had to stop automatically going for the large-sized baggy sweaters in the department stores. This may seem like a simple task, but psychologically, I still saw myself as heavy for quite a while after losing my weight. It took some getting used to. Finally, I was a fit, vibrant, healthy woman.

I have found that what I was feeling is actually quite common. It's as if your mind has a delayed reaction to the reality of your new body. Bonnie Conklin, my children's nanny for the last ten years, has also gone through this physical and mental transformation. She says that she was inspired by my newfound fitness and vitality, and how I totally changed my life. So over the past year, she has lost and kept off over seventy pounds. It's also taken her some time to truly believe what she now sees in the mirror.

Bonnie Conklin, my children's nanny for over ten years, before her weight loss. . .

And after!

BONNIE CONKLIN:

The other day, I was talking to my mom. I mentioned how that morning I'd been in my bathrobe, brushing my hair, and happened to look up in the mirror. And I realized that I had a face. I mean, I always thought my face was round, and all of a sudden I realized . . . I have cheekbones. I have a jawline. My face isn't round, it has a shape to it.

I went on to tell her about a time when my younger brother and I were in high school. We were in the bathroom getting ready, brushing our hair and teeth. He was standing behind me and said, "Bonnie, you would be really pretty if you just lost the weight." That was the closest my brother had ever come to giving me a compliment. And that stuck in my head for years. Why did it take me so long to see what my brother saw?

It always takes us longer to see something in ourselves that is so clear for others to see. It's human nature. We don't like to admit our flaws, and our lack of ego often doesn't allow us to take pride in our assets.

Something I've recently taken up that seems to bring all these things into focus for me is meditation. I'm not talking about the kind of meditation where you sit crossed-

69

legged and chant. I have no plans to travel to India or visit an ashram in the near future. What I'm talking about is a peaceful awareness and the practice of mindful focus.

It's not some mystical experience or anything mysterious. It's really about clearing your mind and becoming almost a spectator to your own thoughts — calmly noticing those thoughts as they occur but refusing to react to them. Stress, you know, is our reaction to our mind's thoughts. Clarity of thought always serves you positively. I'm really talking about relaxation and a form of stress reduction.

If this interests you, I recommend that you pick up a book or an audiotape on meditation. There are a lot of good products out there that can help get you started. You might be surprised to find that your community may even offer some meditation classes. It's become quite mainstream these days.

The power of positive thinking . . . relaxation . . . visualization . . . meditation. You may be asking yourself, "What does any of this have to do with cooking?" And my answer is simple. They're all ingredients in my new healthy lifestyle. And as with any good recipe, there are several ingredients that go into making that recipe work. You can't make chicken soup using only chicken. So it is the recipe to having a healthier, happier life that these pages are offering to you.

Great chefs aren't just born. They study their craft and try to perfect it. They're willing to take risks and experiment with different ingredients until they get it right, and they hold on to the recipes that they know work for them. I hope you find these ingredients helpful in your own journey to fitness, and that in the end, you too will believe anything is possible. After all, I wrote a cookbook.

Finally, I found me . . . isn't life grand?

PART TWO

COOKING TIPS

Stocking Up . . . A Fit Kitchen

One of the things I tried to do in writing this book was to eliminate recipes that call for weird ingredients. If I couldn't find it at my local grocery store, it's not in this book. I have created a list of all the "staples" I think every well-stocked kitchen should contain.

I have split up the list into five categories, starting with the kitchen tools I recommend. If you don't have one already, I encourage you to buy a good set of knives. High-quality sharp knives will help you "cut down" on preparation time, and reduce struggles with chopping, slicing, and dicing.

You certainly don't need to rush out and buy any of these to use my recipes (and you may find you already have most of them), so view these as suggestions, not as "musts":

Kitchen Tools

Set of sharp cook's knives	Selection of skewers
A good knife sharpener	Set of measuring cups
Box grater	Set of measuring spoons
Kitchen scissors	Sieve
Can opener	Wooden spoons
Potato/vegetable peeler	Pasta spoon
Garlic press	Mixing bowls
Good cutting board	Pepper mill

Blender	Hot-air popper
Food processor	Nonstick pans
Double boiler	Steamer
Egg separator	Strainer

Next, here are some food items that are helpful to keep on hand. Again, these are suggestions for your convenience. You don't have to have them all to use my book, and not all may be to your taste — but you may find new favorites here.

Seasonings

Low-sodium salt	Sage
Pepper (white, black)	Boullion cubes (chicken, vegetable, beef)
Lemon pepper	
Cayenne pepper	Onion soup mix
Crushed red pepper	Chili powder
Hot sauce	Packaged dry chili seasoning
Paprika	
Garlic powder	Ground ginger
Garlic salt	Cinnamon
Minced garlic	Soy sauce (preferably low-sodium)
Dill weed	
Oregano	Teriyaki sauce (preferably low-sodium)
Basil leaves	
Cumin	Worcestershire sauce
Dry mustard	Extra-virgin olive oil
Curry powder	Red wine vinegar
Parsley flakes	Balsamic vinegar
Italian seasonings	Vegetable oil
Ground coriander	Nonstick cooking spray (such as PAM)
Thyme	

Perishable Items

Dijon mustard
Low-fat or fat-free
   mayonnaise
Lemons
Fresh garlic

Onions
Parmesan cheese
   (preferably freshly
   grated)
Fresh herbs

Canned Goods

Kidney beans
Black beans
Crushed tomatoes
Tomato sauce

Tomato paste
Stewed tomatoes
Low-sodium chicken
   stock

Pasta/Rice/Grains

Spaghetti
Spaghettini
Linguine
Pasta shells
Penne

Orzo
White rice
Pilaf
Corn meal

If you use this list, you'll always have something in the house to make . . . even when your kids complain, "There's nothing to eat around here!" The idea is to help you get and stay organized.

It also helps to keep your cookware, utensils, and small appliances close to where you use them: your pots and pans near your stove, your food processor (if you have one) near your sink and cutting board, and the stuff you don't often use stored out of sight. Leave yourself room to create.

10 Tips for Quick Healthy Cooking

By Patsy Jamieson, test kitchen director, *Eating Well* magazine, and a *Good Morning America* regular.

1. Choose lean meat cuts, such as beef round or rump steak, rather than chuck; pork tenderloin rather than loin or shoulder; chicken or turkey breasts rather than thighs.

2. When serving meat, poultry, or fish, control the portion size. Allow 4 ounces of raw meat (which will shrink to 3 ounces when cooked) per portion. Use meat as a flavoring rather than the main event, and compensate with additional vegetables and grains.

3. Trim meats carefully of fat. Removing poultry skin saves about 5 grams of fat per 3-ounce portion. If the poultry will be marinated or braised, remove the skin before cooking; but if it will be roasted, remove the skin after cooking.

4. Use canned chicken or vegetable broth to moisten pasta dishes, and even to compensate for some of the oil in salad dressings. Store canned chicken broth in the refrigerator, rather than a cupboard. Then it is easy to remove the fat, which solidifies on the surface.

5. In vinaigrette salad dressings, replace about half of the oil with defatted chicken broth, fruit or vegetable juice, or brewed tea.

6. Because fat not only provides richness but amplifies flavor, it is often necessary to increase seasonings in a low-fat dish. Using whole spices and toasting them before grinding imparts a richer flavor to a dish.

7. Cooking methods such as grilling and high-heat roasting bring out the sweetness in vegetables, such as red onions, asparagus, green beans, tomatoes, and bell peppers. Serve grilled or roasted vegetables as a side dish, in a salad, or toss them with pasta.

8. Pine nuts, walnuts, almonds, and hazelnuts contribute a distinctive flavor and ap-

pealing crunchy texture to salads and desserts. But nuts are a concentrated source of fat, containing about 15 grams of fat per ounce. Rather than eliminating nuts from recipes, use a smaller quantity and toast them to intensify their flavor.

9. In dishes in which cheese plays an integral role, reduce the quantity and use high-quality cheeses that deliver maximum flavor, such as aged Parmigiano-Reggiano or feta.

10. Spend your "fat budget" wisely by selecting the best ingredients available. A small amount of good-quality extra-virgin olive oil will contribute more and better flavor than "light" olive oil, while offering the same amount of fat.

Nutritional Analyses

The recipes that follow were computer-analyzed using Nutritionist 3 software. Here are some tips to help you interpret the information we give with each recipe:

• When a recipe gives a range of servings, such as "Makes 6 to 8 servings," the analysis is for the smaller portion size (in this case, one-eighth of a recipe). Why? We rationalize that the tied-to-the-numbers, nutrition-minded person would opt for the smaller serving.

• When a range of ingredient amounts is given, such as "1 to 1½ pounds chicken breasts," we analyzed the midpoint (here, 1¼ pounds).

• Optional ingredients are not included in the analyses. Lemon slices, for example, weren't included. Garnishes are included if they would logically be eaten with the dish, such as a dollop of sour cream or yogurt spooned onto soup.

• Numbers were rounded for simplicity's sake. For example, 3.2 grams of fat would be listed as 3 grams; 3.5 would be 4 grams.

• When ingredient options are offered, such as "1 teaspoon olive oil, butter, or margarine," analysis was done using the first option — the olive oil. The exception is recipes calling for "homemade chicken stock, chicken broth, or reduced-sodium canned chicken broth." While homemade stock is best, analyses were done using reduced-sodium canned broth, since many time-conscious cooks are apt to use it.

Unfortunately, even the reduced-sodium canned broth adds quite a bit of sodium to the numbers here. The sodium-sensitive person can avoid this problem with homemade broth: simmer a pot of it on weekends, freeze it in ice cube trays, then pop the cubes into freezer bags for later use. Each cube equals about 2 tablespoons of broth. There's no need to thaw — just drop the cubes into your skillet or pan.

• Only a fraction of the marinades, or the amount usually absorbed by meat, was included in analyses.

• Whenever possible, we suggest that you use a homemade tomato sauce, like the recipes we provide on pages 197–98. It will greatly reduce your sodium intake. Understanding that most of us will still use a canned sauce out of convenience, we offer the option in all of the recipes.

Chapter 6

SNACKS AND APPETIZERS

BRUSCHETTA AND CROSTINI

Some people crave sweets. Thank God for small favors that I don't. I do, however, make up for it by loving crunchy munchies. With its toasty bread and tasty toppings, this classic Italian appetizer satisfies that longing for crunchy, salty foods without getting you into trouble. The beauty is in the versatility here. Each time I make these hors d'oeuvres, I vary the toppings. Here are three favorites.

Makes 24 appetizers

24 bruschetta or crostini (recipe follows)
1 recipe marinated tomato, asparagus
*   and Parmesan, or mushroom topping*

BRUSCHETTA AND CROSTINI

Nonstick olive or vegetable oil spray
1 thin baguette or loaf of Italian bread,
*   cut crosswise into ⅓-inch-thick slices*

To make the bruschetta: Prepare a grill or heat a grill pan and spray it with the nonstick olive oil spray. Arrange the bread on the grill 4 inches from the coals (or right on the grill pan if using) and grill it for about 2 minutes a side or until it is lightly browned.

To make the crostini: Arrange the bread in one layer on a baking sheet and toast it in a preheated 400°F. oven for 10 minutes or until it is golden.

Nutritional Analysis *per ⅓-inch slice, untopped: 19 calories; 20% calories from fat; less than ½ gram of fat; 35 milligrams of sodium*

MARINATED TOMATO TOPPING

Makes about ¾ cup

½ pound tomatoes (about 2 medium),
*   seeded and chopped*
½ garlic clove, minced (about ½ teaspoon)
1 teaspoon extra-virgin olive oil
1½ tablespoons shredded fresh basil
Salt and pepper to taste

In a bowl, stir together all the ingredients, and add salt and pepper to taste. Mound a heaping teaspoon of marinated tomatoes on top of each bruschetta or crostini.

Nutritional Analysis *per ½ tablespoon: 43 calories; 16% calories from fat; 1 gram of fat; 79 milligrams of sodium*

ASPARAGUS AND PARMESAN TOPPING

Makes about ¾ cup

*1 bunch medium asparagus (about 12),
the tough ends removed and the stalks
peeled*
Nonstick olive or vegetable oil spray
*1 tablespoon Reduced-Fat Italian Dress-
ing (page 124) or your favorite purchased low-fat or nonfat brand*
1 ounce shaved Parmesan cheese or
freshly grated Parmesan cheese*
Juice of ½ lemon

Preheat the oven to 400°F.

Arrange the asparagus in one layer on a sheet
pan that has been sprayed with the nonstick
olive oil spray. Roast the asparagus in the preheated oven for 10 minutes or until just tender.

Chop the asparagus stalks and cut the tips
in half for garnish. Toss with the dressing.
Arrange one shaving of Parmesan (or a sprinkle
of the grated) on top of each toast. Mound a
heaping teaspoon of the marinated asparagus
stems on top of the cheese, and top it with 2
halves of an asparagus tip. Squeeze a little of the
lemon on top of each mound.

**To shave Parmesan cheese: Using a swivel-bladed vegetable peeler,
peel off paper-thin strips of cheese. This procedure works best if the
Parmesan has been left at room temperature for 20 minutes.*

Nutritional Analysis *per ½ tablespoon: 50 calories; 18% calories from fat; 1 gram of fat; 106 milligrams of sodium*

MUSHROOM TOPPING

Makes about 1 cup

*1 medium onion, chopped fine (about 1
cup)*
2 teaspoons butter or vegetable oil
*½ pound mushrooms (all cultivated, or
any combination of wild and cultivated), wiped clean with a damp cloth
and chopped coarse (or quartered if
small)*
½ teaspoon dried thyme
1 tablespoon dry sherry
*½ cup Chicken Broth (page 203) or
canned reduced-sodium chicken broth*
*1 tablespoon chopped fresh parsley or
chives, optional*
Salt and pepper to taste

In a nonstick pan, cook the onion in the butter over moderately low heat for 5 minutes or
until the onion is softened. Add the mushrooms and cook the mixture over moderate
heat for 5 minutes, or until most of the liquid
the mushrooms give off is evaporated. Add the
thyme, the sherry, and the chicken broth, and
simmer the mixture until it is reduced by half.
Stir in the parsley, if using, and salt and pepper
to taste. Mound a heaping teaspoon on top of
each bruschetta or each of the crostini.

Nutritional Analysis *per 2 teaspoons: 49 calories; 18% calories from fat; 1 gram of fat; 93 milligrams of sodium*

G U I L T L E S S   P O T A T O   S K I N S
W I T H   S A L S A   A N D   C H E E S E

Potato skins are one of my favorite things in life. (Why are all the good things usually fattening? And all of the fattening things good?) Although potatoes have earned a bad reputation among dieters, it's really what you put on the potato that's the problem, not the potato itself. So here I've combined healthier choices to allow me to have my potato skins and eat them, too.

Serves 4

2 large baking potatoes (about 1¼ to 1½
    pounds total), scrubbed
2 teaspoons olive oil
½ recipe Tomato Salsa (page 93) or your
    favorite purchased brand
4 tablespoons shredded low-fat or part-
    skim mozzarella or Monterey Jack
    cheese

Preheat the oven to 425°F.

Prick the potatoes a few times with a knife, and bake them in the preheated oven for 1 hour or until they are tender. Let the potatoes cool until they can be handled. Cut them in half lengthwise and scoop out the potato flesh (reserving it for another use), leaving a ¼-inch-thick shell.

Sprinkle the inside of each shell with ½ teaspoon of the oil. Cut each shell into 3 long strips and arrange them, cut side up, on a baking pan. Broil them 4 inches from the flame for 3 to 4 minutes or until golden; turn them over and broil for 1 minute more on the other side. Turn them cut side up, spread some of the salsa on top of each strip, and top with some of the cheese. Broil the skins just until the cheese is melted.

Note: For a more filling and less crispy potato skin, don't scoop out as much of the potato.

Nutritional Analysis *per serving: 161 calories; 31% calories from fat; 6 grams of fat; 49 milligrams of sodium*

QUESADILLAS

When I come home hungry and I'm in a hurry, this snack's a lifesaver. I always keep tortillas and low-fat shredded cheese in the house so I can make this quick and easy snack. For my kids, I keep them simple, but you can spice them up with hot green chili peppers — or not, for the heat resistant. (Wimps!) If you're really in a hurry, stick them in the microwave oven, like I do. Corn tortillas contain even less fat than flour tortillas, in case you're watching every gram.

Serves 4

1 cup shredded low-fat Monterey Jack or
    mozzarella cheese
4 six-inch flour tortillas
Nonstick vegetable oil spray
4 teaspoons low-fat sour cream

OPTIONAL ADDITIONS:
3 tablespoons minced onion or scallion
8 sun-dried tomatoes (not oil-packed), re-
    hydrated*
½ cup shredded cooked chicken
½ cup Quick Chili Beans (page 196)

Spread one-quarter of the cheese on the bottom half of each tortilla. Spray a large nonstick pan with some of the vegetable spray, and heat it over moderately high heat. Add the tortillas (in batches if necessary) and gently fold over the top of each one to enclose the cheese, pressing down the tortilla with a spatula. Cook them for 2 minutes a side, or until they are just golden.

Transfer them to a baking sheet and keep them warm in a slow oven while you cook the rest. Cut each quesadilla into four pieces, and garnish with the sour cream.

Note: To add any of the optional ingredients to the recipe, just mix it in a bowl with the cheese before stuffing the tortillas.

To rehydrate sun-dried tomatoes: Pour boiling water over the tomatoes (to cover) and let them stand for 20 minutes. Drain and pat dry.

Nutritional Analysis *per serving: 180 calories; 30% calories from fat; 6 grams of fat; 252 milligrams of sodium*

OVEN-BAKED ROSEMARY CHIPS

Sara Moulton

These homemade potato chips aren't fried. In fact, they're so good I'll bet you can't eat just one. This is a favorite recipe of Sara Moulton, who helped with all of the recipes in this book. I, of course, get to see her bright, smiling face early in the morning when she prepares the recipes for chefs visiting *Good Morning America*. And some people think *I'm* perky. . . .

Makes about 180 (serving 8 to 10)

3 baking potatoes (about 2 to 2¼ pounds
   total), scrubbed
Nonstick olive or vegetable oil spray
Salt to taste
Dried rosemary for sprinkling
Seasoning alternatives: dried thyme,
   dried Italian herbs

Preheat the oven to 350°F.

Using a mandoline or hand-held slicer, very thinly slice the potatoes crosswise (about ⅛ inch thick). Spray several sheet pans well with the nonstick olive oil spray, and arrange the potato slices in a single layer on top. Spray the top of the potatoes lightly with the olive oil spray, and bake them in the preheated oven for 15 to 20 minutes or until they are golden. (They may brown at different rates, so just remove the ones that are done and put the rest back in the oven.) Transfer the chips to a pan lined with paper towels, and sprinkle them while they are hot with salt (to taste) and rosemary, or one of the seasoning alternatives.

Nutritional Analysis *per 18-chip serving: 111 calories; 1% calories from fat; trace amount of fat; 72 milligrams of sodium*

SWEET POTATO OVEN FRIES

What? A snack that sneaks vitamin A into your diet (three times your daily requirement) and only a trace of fat? Even kids who might not go for sweet potatoes will ask for these. I, personally, would eat a sweet potato no matter which way you cooked it.

Serves 4

2 medium sweet potatoes (about 1¼ to
  1½ pounds total), scrubbed
Nonstick vegetable oil spray
Salt to taste

OPTIONAL SEASONINGS:
Mix equal parts ground nutmeg and cinnamon
Mix ⅛ teaspoon each: paprika, garlic
  flakes, and salt with a pinch of
  cayenne pepper

Preheat the oven to 400°F.

Cut the potatoes crosswise, ¼ inch thick. Spray a baking sheet with the nonstick vegetable oil spray and arrange the potatoes in one layer. Bake them in the preheated oven for 15 minutes, turn them over, and bake them for an additional 10 minutes or until just golden. Sprinkle them with salt or with one of the optional seasonings, if desired.

Nutritional Analysis *per serving: 125 calories; 1% calories from fat; trace amount of fat; 65 milligrams of sodium*

FAT-FREE FRENCH FRIES

Show me a person who doesn't like french fries and we'll swap lies. To me, a wish come true is a fat-free french fry. Thanks to Sara Moulton for granting me my wish.

Serves 4

3 baking potatoes (about 2 to 2¼ pounds total), scrubbed
Nonstick olive or vegetable oil spray
Salt to taste

Preheat the oven to 350°F.

Cut the potatoes into french fry–size pieces, about ⅓ inch thick and 1½ to 2 inches long. Spray a sheet pan with the nonstick olive oil spray, and arrange the potato sticks in one layer on the pan. Bake the potatoes in the preheated oven for 20 minutes. Brown them in a preheated broiler, turning them until they are crispy on all sides. Sprinkle with salt, if desired.

Nutritional Analysis *per serving: 278 calories; 1% calories from fat; trace amount of fat; 74 milligrams of sodium*

PITA CHIPS

Crunchy is my weakness, so you'll hear a lot of crunching between these book covers. Legal crunching. I'm also a pushover for anything salty. I know lots of salt is not good for you. On these pita chips and tortilla chips, the salt can be replaced with a sprinkling of spices.

Makes 64 chips (8 per serving)

4 six-inch pita pockets
Nonstick olive oil spray or 1 tablespoon
*   olive oil*
Salt to taste

OPTIONAL SEASONINGS:
cayenne, ground cumin, dried rosemary,
*   chopped fresh dill*

Preheat the oven to 350°F.

Split the pita pockets to form 8 single rounds. Lightly spray or brush the rounds with the olive oil, cut each one into 8 wedges, and bake them on a sheet pan in the preheated oven for 8 minutes or until golden and crisp. Sprinkle with salt and one of the optional seasonings, if desired.

Nutritional Analysis *per serving: 53 calories; 5% calories from fat; trace amount of fat; 134 milligrams of sodium*

T O R T I L L A   C H I P S

Makes 64 chips (8 per serving)

8 seven-inch corn tortillas
Nonstick vegetable or olive oil spray, if
   desired
Salt to taste

OPTIONAL SEASONINGS:
chili powder, ground cumin, cayenne

Preheat the oven to 350°F.

Spray the tortillas lightly with the nonstick vegetable oil spray (if using). Cut each one into 8 wedges, and bake them in the preheated oven for 8 to 10 minutes or until lightly toasted and crispy. Sprinkle lightly with salt and one of the optional seasonings, if desired.

Nutritional Analysis *per serving: 67 calories; 15% calories from fat; 1 gram of fat; 80 milligrams of sodium*

HUMMUS (CHICKPEA SPREAD)

Only after I moved to New York City did I discover hummus, a traditional Middle Eastern chick-pea dip usually served with pocket or pita bread. Unlike *hummus bi tahini,* this version skips the sesame paste, cutting some of the usual fat.

Makes about 2 cups

4 scallions, white part only, chopped
  coarse
19-ounce can of chickpeas (about 2 cups),
  drained and rinsed
¼ teaspoon ground cumin
½ teaspoon ground coriander
2 tablespoons fresh lemon juice
2 tablespoons extra-virgin olive oil
1 or 2 garlic cloves, minced (about 1 to 2
  teaspoons), optional
4 to 6 dashes hot sauce, optional
Salt and pepper to taste
4 to 6 tablespoons water
1 recipe Pita Chips (page 88)

Puree the first eight ingredients in a food processor, then add salt and pepper to taste. With the processor motor running, add enough water to achieve a nice dipping consistency. Serve with the Pita Chips.

Nutritional Analysis *per 2 tablespoons: 38 calories; 48% calories from fat; 2 grams of fat; 89 milligrams of sodium*

SPINACH DIP

Prepackaged spinach makes this reduced-fat version of the classic spinach dip truly convenient.

Makes about 1½ cups

10-ounce package fresh spinach, coarse
    stems removed, rinsed well but not
    dried
½ cup low-fat or nonfat sour cream or
    nonfat plain yogurt
4 ounces low-fat ricotta cheese (about ½
    cup)
2 to 2½ tablespoons fresh lemon juice or
    to taste
2 tablespoons chopped fresh dill
½ teaspoon grated nutmeg
Salt to taste
½ teaspoon freshly ground black pepper
2 tablespoons water

OPTIONAL SEASONINGS:
½ teaspoon dried tarragon or fennel seeds
    in place of the dill
1 garlic clove, minced (about 1 teaspoon)
½ teaspoon red pepper flakes

In a large pot, steam the spinach over high heat, covered, in the water left clinging to its leaves for 3 to 5 minutes, or until it is wilted. Drain, rinse it under cold water (this will set the color), and squeeze out the excess water with your hands. Puree the spinach in a food processor with the remaining ingredients and any of the optional seasonings, if desired, until it is smooth. Serve with Pita Chips or raw veggies.

Nutritional Analysis *per 2 tablespoons: 18 calories; 18% calories from fat; trace amount of fat; 27 milligrams of sodium*

GUACAMOLE

Guacamole is high in fat and calories because avocados — the principal ingredient — are high in fat. Naturally, that's why they taste so buttery, darn it. Too much fat, no matter what kind, can raise your blood cholesterol, according to the experts. Excess fat also can make you shaped like an avocado. However, most of the fat in avocados is monounsaturated, like olive oil, which isn't thought to raise blood cholesterol and contribute to heart disease. That's better than choosing a saturated fat, the biggest dietary no-no. This has half the fat, or less, of the classic guacamoles, and was given to me by cookbook author Marie Simmons.

Makes about 2 cups

1 ripe avocado, peeled, halved, and pitted
1 cup chopped, seeded plum or cherry tomatoes
½ cup chopped seedless cucumber
¼ cup chopped scallion
2 tablespoons fresh lime juice
2 tablespoons chopped fresh coriander
1 tablespoon seeded, minced jalapeño or hot sauce to taste, optional
1 garlic clove, minced (about 1 teaspoon), optional
Salt to taste
1 recipe Tortilla Chips (page 89) or Pita Chips (page 88)

In a large bowl, mash the avocado with a fork. Stir in all but the last of the other ingredients and salt to taste. Serve with the Tortilla Chips or Pita Chips.

Nutritional Analysis *per 2 tablespoons, not including chips: 24 calories; 66% calories from fat; 2 grams of fat; 3 milligrams of sodium*

Nutritional Analysis *per 2 tablespoons, including 4 Tortilla Chips: 58 calories; 37% calories from fat; 3 grams of fat; 43 milligrams of sodium*

TOMATO SALSA

With not a trace of added fat, this salsa is the ultimate in skinny dips — less than ⅒ of a gram of fat per 2 tablespoons.

Makes about 2 cups

1 pound tomatoes (about 4 medium), seeded and chopped
1 small onion, chopped fine (about ½ cup), or ½ cup chopped scallion
1 garlic clove, minced (about 1 teaspoon)
1 fresh or pickled jalapeño or to taste, seeded and minced, or 1 teaspoon hot sauce
1 to 2 tablespoons fresh lime juice or to taste
2 tablespoons chopped fresh coriander or fresh basil or to taste
Salt to taste

In a bowl, toss together all the ingredients with salt to taste. Chill for 30 minutes, covered, to develop the flavor.

Nutritional Analysis *per 2 tablespoons: 9 calories; 9% calories from fat; trace amount of fat; 3 milligrams of sodium*

HEALTHY PIZZA

Everyone thinks of kids when they think of pizza. But let's be honest, I think all of us, especially us kids at heart, really adore pizza. It has become our national comfort food. This lower-fat version tastes as good as the more familiar kinds, but with fewer calories and fat. It's also super fast and super easy. What more can you ask for? Use leftover cooked meats and vegetables as toppings.

Makes 6 individual pizzas

1 package dry yeast
Pinch of sugar
1 cup lukewarm water
1½ cups whole wheat flour
1½ cups all-purpose flour plus additional
  for dusting the board
1 teaspoon salt
¾ cup Tomato Sauce (pages 197–198) or
  your favorite purchased brand
6 ounces low-fat mozzarella cheese,
  coarsely grated

OPTIONAL TOPPINGS:
Sliced zucchini
Sliced red, yellow, or green peppers
Sliced mushrooms
Chopped fresh herbs (such as basil, pars-
  ley, dill, oregano, or chives)

Preheat the oven to 500°F.

In a small bowl, proof the yeast with the sugar in ¼ cup of the water, tightly covered, for 5 minutes or until the yeast is foamy. Transfer the yeast mixture to a bowl, stir in the additional water, the flours, and salt and combine well. Turn the dough out onto a lightly floured board and knead it (adding additional flour or water as necessary) for 10 minutes or until it is smooth and elastic. Put it in a lightly oiled bowl, turn it to coat it with the oil, and let it rise, tightly covered, in a warm place for 1 hour or until it is double in bulk.

Shape the dough into 6 balls and roll out each into a 5-inch round for a thick crust or a 9-inch round for a thin crust. Transfer the rounds to cookie sheets, and spread 2 tablespoons of the tomato sauce on top of each one. Arrange any optional toppings over the sauce, and sprinkle with one-sixth of the cheese.

Bake on the bottom of the preheated oven for 10 to 12 minutes or until the crust is golden on the bottom.

Note: To make the recipe with rapid-rise yeast, mix 1 package of the rapid-rise yeast with the dry ingredients, stir in the water, and knead for 10 minutes or until it is smooth and elastic. Put it in a lightly oiled bowl, turn to coat it with the oil, and let it rise, tightly covered, in a warm place for 30 minutes or until it is double in bulk.

Nutritional Analysis *per pizza, without optional toppings: 288 calories; 11% calories from fat; 4 grams of fat; 433 milligrams of sodium*

BIKER BILLY'S RED-HOT PEPPER SALSA

Biker Billy

I'll never forget the morning Biker Billy arrived with twelve biker friends at the *Good Morning America* studio. Even though I was upstairs in makeup, I could hear their engines roaring as they made their way onto the set. As I donned a black leather motorcycle jacket, Biker Billy whipped up his hot, and I do mean hot, salsa. Grab a hose, dip some chips, and enjoy. Don't be alarmed by the high percentage of calories from fat. Because the total ingredients are low in calories and fat, the 1 tablespoon of oil contributes the bulk of both.

Makes about 1½ to 1¾ cups

1 or more fresh long slim red cayenne
   peppers, stemmed and minced
1 medium onion, chopped (about 1 cup)
1 red bell pepper, diced
1 tablespoon extra-virgin olive oil
½ teaspoon freshly ground pepper
½ teaspoon salt or to taste
1 cup water

In a large nonstick skillet, cook the cayenne peppers, onion, and red bell pepper in the oil over moderate heat for 5 minutes or until the onion is softened. Add the ground pepper, salt, and water, bring the mixture to a boil and simmer it, covered, for 10 minutes.

Transfer the mixture to a blender or food processor, and puree it for 10 to 15 seconds or until no large pieces of pepper remain. Serve warm.

Note: For variety, substitute 1 cup diced roasted red bell pepper for the fresh bell pepper.

Nutritional Analysis *per 2 tablespoons: 15 calories; 58% calories from fat; 1 gram of fat; 77 milligrams of sodium*

Chapter 7

SOUPS

CREAMY CARROT SOUP

Don't be scared away by the word *creamy.* There's no cream in this soup, but your taste buds will swear it's lurking in there, just waiting to settle on your hips. But they've been fooled, and your hips spared.

Makes about 6 cups

1 medium onion, chopped (about 1 cup)
1 or 2 garlic cloves, minced (about 1 to 2
   teaspoons)
2 teaspoons vegetable oil or unsalted butter
3 cups Chicken Broth (page 203) or
   canned reduced-sodium chicken broth
6 carrots, thinly sliced
2 parsnips, thinly sliced
½ teaspoon dried thyme
1 tablespoon fresh lemon juice
1 tablespoon tomato paste or ¼ cup V-8
   Juice
4 drops hot sauce
¼ cup nonfat plain yogurt
1 to 2 cups water, or as needed
Salt and pepper to taste
Chopped fresh dill and lemon slices for
   garnish, optional

In a saucepan, cook the onion and the garlic in the oil over moderately low heat for 5 minutes or until the onions are softened. Add the broth, carrots, parsnips, and thyme; bring to a boil; and simmer for 30 minutes or until the vegetables are very tender.

Transfer the mixture to a blender or food processor, in batches, and puree until smooth. Add the remaining ingredients, salt and pepper to taste, and enough water to achieve the desired consistency, and blend the mixture.

Serve hot or chilled. Garnish each portion with the dill and lemon slices, if desired.

Nutritional Analysis *per 1-cup serving: 106 calories; 20% calories from fat; 2 grams of fat; 406 milligrams of sodium*

B U T T E R N U T   S Q U A S H   S O U P

I happen to really enjoy butternut squash — a good source of vitamin A, by the way. So here is a recipe that is both good and nutritious. This one, in fact, gives you your whole day's vitamin A, and almost a third of your daily vitamin C requirement. Serve as a first course, or the soup can take center stage at lunch or a light supper.

Makes about 6 cups

1 medium butternut squash (about 2¼
    pounds)
Nonstick vegetable oil spray
1 medium onion, chopped (about 1 cup)
1 tablespoon freshly grated ginger, op-
    tional
1 tablespoon unsalted butter
3 cups Chicken Broth (page 203) or
    canned reduced-sodium chicken broth
1 to 2 cups water, or as needed
Salt and pepper to taste
Low-fat or nonfat sour cream and apple
    slices for garnish, optional

Preheat the oven to 400°F.

Cut the squash in half lengthwise, and scoop out and discard the seeds. Arrange the halves cut side down in a roasting pan that has been sprayed with the nonstick vegetable oil spray. Bake the squash in the oven for 40 to 45 minutes or until it is very tender. Set aside to cool.

When the squash is completely cool, scoop the flesh from the skin.

While the squash is baking, cook the onion and the ginger (if using) in the butter in a saucepan, over moderately low heat, for 5 minutes or until the onion is softened. Add the broth and simmer the mixture for 10 minutes, covered. Add the squash pulp to the saucepan.

Transfer the mixture to a blender or a food processor, in batches, and puree until smooth. Add enough water to achieve the desired consistency, and salt and pepper to taste. Return the soup to the saucepan and cook it over moderate heat until it is hot.

Garnish each portion with a heaping teaspoon of low-fat sour cream and a few apple slices, if desired.

Nutritional Analysis *per 1-cup serving: 85 calories; 25% calories from fat; 3 grams of fat; 354 milligrams of sodium*

SPICY CHICKEN TORTILLA SOUP

Living in Mexico City for three-and-a-half years during college, I fell for tortilla soup, a classic recipe that you can't appreciate on paper as much as when you're eating it. During those college years, tortilla soup and I had a love affair. I simply couldn't live each week without it.

Makes about 7 cups

1 medium onion, chopped (about 1 cup)
2 garlic cloves, minced (about 2 teaspoons)
2 tablespoons vegetable oil
4-ounce can green chilies, chopped
15-ounce can Italian-style stewed tomatoes, chopped, reserving the juice
4 cups Chicken Broth (page 203) or
   canned reduced-sodium chicken broth
1 teaspoon lemon pepper
2 teaspoons Worcestershire sauce
1 teaspoon chili powder
1 teaspoon ground cumin
½ teaspoon hot sauce or to taste
4 tablespoons all-purpose flour
½ cup water
1 pound skinless boneless chicken breast,
   cut into small cubes
⅓ cup nonfat or low-fat sour cream
Salt and pepper to taste
Tortilla Strips (recipe follows)
Chopped fresh coriander for garnish, optional

In a large saucepan, cook the onion and the garlic in the oil over moderately low heat for 5 minutes or until the onion is softened. Add the chilies, tomatoes with their juice, broth, lemon pepper, Worcestershire, spices, and hot sauce and simmer the mixture for 20 minutes.

In a small bowl, combine the flour with the water and whisk it into the soup. Bring the soup back to a boil and simmer for 5 minutes. Add the chicken and simmer for 5 minutes or until it is just cooked through. Stir in the sour cream and salt and pepper to taste, and garnish each portion with the tortilla strips and the co-riander, if desired.

Nutritional Analysis *per 1-cup serving, including Tortilla Strips: 219 calories; 29% calories from fat; 7 grams of fat; 943 milligrams of sodium*

TORTILLA STRIPS

4 corn tortillas cut into ¼-inch strips
Nonstick vegetable oil spray

Preheat the oven to 400°F.

Arrange the tortilla strips in one layer in a baking pan sprayed with vegetable oil. Bake them in the oven for 10 minutes or until they are lightly toasted and crispy. Sprinkle lightly with salt, if desired.

GRANDMA JOIE'S CHICKEN SOUP

Joie Krauss

I'm a firm believer in the theory that chicken soup is a cure-all. Best of all, you don't even have to be sick to enjoy it. My former mother-in-law, Joie Krauss, with whom I speak frequently, offered this recipe. When I get in a real jam in the kitchen, I always call Grandma Joie. Like she says, a little chicken soup may not help, but it sure never hurts.

Makes 10 to 12 cups

3½-pound chicken (preferably kosher), rinsed and cut up
1 large onion, cut into eighths
1 large carrot, halved
1 stalk celery, halved
1 large parsnip, halved
1 small bunch parsley
Salt and pepper to taste
Boiled white rice or cooked matzo balls (prepared according to package instructions), optional

In a large kettle, combine the chicken with cold water to cover by 2 inches. Bring the water to a boil and simmer, skimming the scum that rises to the surface. Simmer the soup for 20 minutes, skimming as needed, and add the vegetables and parsley. Bring the soup back to a boil and simmer for 2 hours. Strain the stock, skim off the fat, and remove the meat from the bones, discarding the bones. In the cleaned kettle combine the stock with the chicken, add salt and pepper to taste, and cook the mixture over moderate heat until it is hot. Ladle over the optional ingredients, if using.

Nutritional Analysis *per 1-cup serving: 85 calories; 25% calories from fat; 2 grams of fat; 36 milligrams of sodium*

JEFF'S POTATO CHOWDER
WITH LEEKS

Potatoes are among my top ten favorite vegetables. Since my brother is amazingly adept in the kitchen, I turned to him for this wonderful chowder. It's a cousin to the classic cold vichyssoise, which is usually laden with whipping cream, adding lots of fat and calories.

Jeff Blunden

Makes about 10 cups

5 large baking potatoes (about 3 to 3½ pounds), peeled and cut into ¼-inch cubes
4 medium leeks, white part only, minced (about 2 cups), rinsed well and patted dry
2 tablespoons unsalted butter
2 cups Chicken Broth (page 203) or canned reduced-sodium chicken broth
2 to 3 cups water, or as needed
¼ to ½ teaspoon hot sauce, or to taste
½ to 1 teaspoon Worcestershire, or to taste
½ cup 1% milk
½ cup nonfat or low-fat sour cream
Salt and pepper to taste
1 bunch chives, chopped

Peel and dice the potatoes. In a large pot combine the potatoes with enough water to cover. Bring to a boil and simmer, covered, for 20 to 30 minutes or until tender.

In a large nonstick skillet, cook the leeks in the butter over moderately low heat for 5 minutes or until they are softened. Drain the potatoes and return them to the pot. Add the broth and 2 cups of the water and heat. Transfer the mixture to a blender, in batches, and puree about three-fourths of it. (Some of the cubes should be left for texture.) Do not overblend or the soup will be gluey. Add the leeks, hot sauce, Worcestershire, milk, sour cream and salt and pepper (preferably white — black will show as flecks in the soup) to taste, and heat the soup until it is hot. Stir in some of the additional water, if necessary, to achieve the desired consistency.

Serve hot or chilled. (If chilled it may be necessary to thin with additional water.) Garnish each portion with chopped chives.

Nutritional Analysis *per 1-cup serving: 219 calories; 13% calories from fat; 3 grams of fat; 316 milligrams of sodium*

HUNGARIAN GOULASH SOUP

Goulash is one of the all-time great foods. This slimmed-down version gives you all of the taste and robust flavor of a traditional goulash, without all of the unwanted fat and calories. I like it over noodles, and my nutritionist recommends that I use a no-yolk noodle to make it more healthful.

Makes about 8 cups

2 tablespoons olive or vegetable oil
1 pound pork tenderloin, cut into ½-inch
    cubes
2 medium onions, chopped (about 2 cups)
4 garlic cloves, minced (about 4 tea-
    spoons)
2 tablespoons all-purpose flour
2 tablespoons paprika
1 cup dry white wine
2 tablespoons tomato paste
1 red or green bell pepper, chopped
1 pound boiling potatoes, cut into ½-inch
    cubes
6 cups Chicken Broth (page 203) or
    canned reduced-sodium chicken broth
Salt and pepper to taste
¼ cup low-fat or nonfat sour cream for
    garnish, optional

In a large nonstick skillet, heat the oil over moderately high heat until it is hot. Add the pork, in batches if necessary, and brown it on all sides. Transfer the pork with a slotted spoon to a large saucepan. Add the onions and the garlic to the skillet and cook them over moderate heat for 8 minutes, or until golden. Stir in the flour and the paprika and cook the mixture, stirring, for 2 minutes. Whisk in the wine, bring the mixture to a boil, and transfer it to the saucepan. Add the tomato paste, the pepper, the potato, and the broth and bring the mixture to a boil. Simmer the soup for 1 hour or until the pork is very tender, and add salt and pepper to taste. Garnish each portion with some of the sour cream, if desired.

Note: Serve this soup over boiled egg noodles (regular or yolk-free) to make it a main course.

Nutritional Analysis *per 1-cup serving: 223 calories; 27% calories from fat; 7 grams of fat; 588 milligrams of sodium*

CREAMY TOMATO SOUP

As a little girl, whenever I was hungry on a cold and rainy day, my mom always knew that tomato soup would warm me up. Moms are always right. I still like to eat this soup in the midafternoon, especially when I come home from the studio. Always was a favorite, and still is. Make a large pot and freeze the leftovers for a rainy day.

Makes about 10 cups

1 medium onion, chopped (about 1 cup)
2 garlic cloves, minced (about 2 teaspoons)
1 tablespoon olive or vegetable oil
28-ounce can whole plum tomatoes, chopped, reserving the juice
29-ounce can tomato puree
1 large baking potato, peeled and cubed
2 cups Chicken Broth (page 203) or canned reduced-sodium chicken broth
2 cups 1% milk
Salt and pepper to taste
¼ cup chopped fresh herbs (such as basil, dill, tarragon, or chives) for garnish
½ cup plain low-fat yogurt for garnish, optional

In a large saucepan, cook the onion and the garlic in the oil over moderate heat for 5 minutes or until softened. Add the tomatoes with their juice, the tomato puree, potato and chicken broth and simmer, covered, for 30 minutes or until the potatoes are tender. Puree the mixture in batches in a blender or food processor, and return the soup to the cleaned pan. Whisk in the milk and salt and pepper to taste, and heat the soup over moderate heat until it is hot. Garnish each portion with the herbs and the yogurt, if desired.

Note: This soup may also be served chilled. If chilled, it may be necessary to thin with water.

Nutritional Analysis *per 1-cup serving: 105 calories; 19% calories from fat; 2 grams of fat; 622 milligrams of sodium*

L E N T I L   S O U P

What do you feed a teenage vegetarian? This recipe was a major hit with my sixteen-year-old daughter Jamie. You can vary this recipe greatly, depending on what you have stocked in your pantry. You can add canned or frozen corn, peas, or your favorite beans.

Makes 6 to 7 cups

1 medium onion, chopped (about 1 cup)
2 garlic cloves, minced (about 2 tea-
    spoons)
1 tablespoon olive or vegetable oil
3 carrots, chopped (about 1¼ cups)
2 stalks celery, chopped (about ⅔ cup)
1 cup dried lentils (about 6 ounces),
    picked over and rinsed
5 cups Vegetable Stock (page 204),
    Chicken Broth (page 203), canned
    reduced-sodium chicken broth, or water
1 cup peeled and chopped tomato (fresh
    or canned)
Salt and pepper to taste

OPTIONAL SEASONINGS:
1 teaspoon ground cumin (add with the
    stock)
1 teaspoon fresh lemon juice and 1 tea-
    spoon oregano (add with the tomatoes)
1 tablespoon chopped fresh dill (add at
    the end)

In a large saucepan, cook the onion and the garlic in the oil over moderately low heat for 5 minutes or until they are softened. Add the carrots, celery, lentils, and broth; bring the soup to a boil; and simmer for 30 minutes. Add the tomatoes and salt and pepper to taste, and simmer for 10 minutes or until the lentils are tender.

Nutritional Analysis *per 1-cup serving: 157 calories; 18% calories from fat; 3 grams of fat; 530 milligrams of sodium*

ITALIAN MINESTRONE

With all of these vegetables, this is a naturally low-fat soup with a hearty taste. With a nice loaf of fresh bread, it makes a great light meal.

Makes 10 cups

1 medium onion, chopped (about 1 cup)
4 garlic cloves, minced (about 4 teaspoons)
2 tablespoons olive oil
8 cups Chicken Broth (page 203), Vegetable Stock (page 204), or canned reduced-sodium chicken broth
2 cups water
1 cup defrosted frozen lima beans
½ to 1 teaspoon dried oregano, or to taste
½ to 1 teaspoon dried rosemary, or to taste
14-ounce can Italian plum tomatoes, chopped, juice reserved
2 tablespoons tomato paste
½ pound boiling potatoes, scrubbed and cut into ¼-inch pieces
½ cup dried macaroni shells
3 medium carrots, chopped (about 1¼ cups)
3 stalks celery, chopped (about 1 cup)
1 medium leek, chopped (about ½ cup), rinsed well, and patted dry
1 small zucchini, cut into ¼-inch pieces

½ cup fresh or defrosted frozen peas
Salt and pepper to taste
⅓ cup chopped fresh parsley or basil, optional
½ cup freshly grated Parmesan cheese, optional

In a large kettle, cook the onion and the garlic in the oil over moderately low heat for 10 minutes. Add the broth, the water, the lima beans, and the spices. Bring the mixture to a boil and simmer it for 20 minutes. Add the tomatoes with their juice, tomato paste, potatoes, macaroni, carrots and celery, and simmer for 10 minutes. Add the leek, zucchini, and peas, and simmer for 5 minutes or until they are just tender. Add salt and pepper to taste and the parsley or basil, if using. Serve each portion sprinkled with 2 teaspoons of the Parmesan, if desired.

Nutritional Analysis *per 1-cup serving: 145 calories; 24% calories from fat; 4 grams of fat; 680 milligrams of sodium*

ELISE'S BROCCOLI SOUP

Elise Silvestri

Another versatile soup. Make it creamy by putting it through the food processor, or leave it with colorful chunks of broccoli. It provides a whole day's worth of vitamin C, even in just a cup. What a deal.

Makes about 10 cups

2 pounds broccoli (about 1½ bunches)
2 medium onions, chopped (about 2 cups)
3 stalks celery, chopped (about 1 cup)
1 garlic clove, minced (about 1 teaspoon)
3 tablespoons unsalted butter
½ cup all-purpose flour
½ teaspoon dried thyme
½ teaspoon dried marjoram
4 cups Chicken Broth (page 203) or
*   canned low-sodium chicken broth,*
*   heated*
4 cups 1% milk
Salt and pepper to taste
1 medium tomato, seeded and chopped,
*   for garnish*

Peel the stalks of the broccoli, and cut them into ½-inch lengths. Break the tops into small florets. Steam the broccoli for 5 minutes or until it is crisp tender. Plunge it into cold water to cool it off and drain it.

In a large saucepan, cook the onion, celery, and garlic in the butter over moderately low heat for 5 minutes or until the onion is softened. Add the flour and the herbs and cook the mixture, stirring, for 5 minutes. Whisk in the broth in a stream. Bring the mixture to a boil, whisking. Simmer the mixture for 5 minutes and add the milk. Heat the soup until it is hot, but do not let it boil. Add the broccoli, and salt and pepper to taste, and cook the mixture until it is heated through. Serve each portion with a spoonful of the chopped tomato.

Note: If a smooth texture is desired, this soup may be transferred to a food processor or blender and pureed.

Nutritional Analysis *per 1-cup serving: 146 calories; 31% calories from fat; 5 grams of fat; 363 milligrams of sodium*

Chapter 8

SALADS

DANIEL BOULUD'S MAINE CRAB SALAD WITH MINT/CORIANDER DRESSING

Daniel Boulud is one of the finest chefs in New York City and owner of his namesake restaurant, Daniel. He was kind enough to offer this delicious recipe to us, so we can share it with you.

Serves 4 to 6

Daniel Boulud

8 mint leaves
12 coriander leaves
1 pound fresh Maine crabmeat
2 tablespoons fresh lime juice
3 tablespoons olive oil
8 drops hot sauce
Salt and pepper to taste
1 firm-ripe medium mango, peeled,
    seeded, and cut into ¼-inch dice
    (about 2 cups)
1 cucumber, peeled, seeded, and cut into
    ¼-inch dice (about 1 cup)
1 tablespoon crushed, toasted, unsalted
    peanuts

Reserve 4 leaves each of the mint and coriander and finely chop the rest. In a bowl, toss the crabmeat with half the lime juice, half the oil, two-thirds of the chopped herbs, 4 drops of the hot sauce, and salt and pepper to taste. Arrange on the bottom of a glass bowl.

In another bowl, toss the mango and cucumber with the remaining lime juice, oil, chopped herbs, hot sauce, and salt and pepper to taste. Arrange the mixture evenly on top of the crabmeat. Sprinkle with the peanuts and garnish with the whole herb leaves. Serve well chilled.

Nutritional Analysis *per serving: 166 calories; 46% calories from fat; 9 grams of fat; 354 milligrams of sodium*

SHARON TYLER HERBST'S
SUMMER BREAD SALAD

I remember the day that cookbook author Sharon Tyler Herbst made this dish on *Good Morning America*. It seemed so easy, and tastes incredibly good. Similar to classic Florentine panzanella bread salad, this one's ideal for a dinner party, or just a special dinner with your family.

Sharon Tyler Herbst

Serves 8

FOR THE DRESSING:

2 tablespoons minced shallots
1 tablespoon finely grated lemon rind
1 garlic clove, minced (about 1 teaspoon)
½ teaspoon salt
¼ cup extra-virgin olive oil
3 tablespoons balsamic vinegar
Freshly ground black pepper to taste

FOR THE SALAD:

1 medium cucumber (about ½ pound),
*   peeled if necessary, seeded, and coarsely*
*   chopped*
1 cup finely chopped fresh fennel
2 medium tomatoes, seeded and coarsely
*   chopped*
2 medium bell peppers (red, green, purple,
*   yellow, or orange), coarsely chopped*
½ cup packed fresh basil leaves (green or
*   opal), shredded*
3 cups ½-inch croutons (recipe below)
1 small red onion, sliced thin and sepa-
*   rated into rings*
⅓ cup small imported black olives, such
*   as Niçoise, optional*

Make the dressing: In a large bowl use a fork to mix together shallots, lemon rind, garlic, and salt, mashing the ingredients to release their essence. Whisk in oil, vinegar, and freshly ground black pepper to taste.

Make the salad: Add the cucumber, fennel, tomatoes, peppers, and basil to the bowl and toss well to coat with the dressing. Add the croutons, and toss again. Let stand at room temperature for 30 minutes before serving. Garnish with onion rings and olives, if using.

Note: All the parts of this salad can be prepared ahead of time and then just mixed together 30 minutes before serving.

To make your own croutons: Cut sliced country-style bread into ¾-inch cubes and bake in a preheated 350°F. oven for 7 to 10 minutes or until they are just crisp. (They will shrink in size.)

Nutritional Analysis *per serving: 147 calories; 45% calories from fat; 8 grams of fat; 236 milligrams of sodium*

ORANGE AND BLACK OLIVE SALAD

I'd seen a number of different recipes for this traditional Mediterranean salad, and was always intrigued by the combination of ingredients. The first night that I tried my version on some friends, it was a huge hit! I happen to think that arugula's interesting, but you can use any kind of lettuce you like, or even mixed greens.

Serves 4

4 juicy oranges
¼ cup chopped fresh mint
1 tablespoon extra-virgin olive oil
½ to 1 garlic clove, minced (about ½ to 1 teaspoon), or to taste
½ teaspoon ground coriander
Pinch of cayenne, optional
Pinch of sugar
Salt to taste
1 large bunch of arugula, stems removed, rinsed well and spun dry
2 tablespoons sliced pitted black olives (either Californian or Mediterranean)
1 cup ½-inch croutons (to make your own, see page 111)

With a serrated knife, cut away orange peels and pith and discard, and cut oranges crosswise into thin slices. In a bowl toss the slices gently with the mint, olive oil, garlic, coriander, cayenne (if using), sugar, and salt to taste. Line the bottom of a platter with the arugula. Arrange the oranges on top, overlapping the slices. Sprinkle the olives over the oranges, and serve each portion topped with one-fourth of the croutons.

Nutritional Analysis *per serving: 171 calories; 36% calories from fat; 7 grams of fat; 138 milligrams of sodium*

CAESAR SALAD

I love Caesar salad, and so do my kids. My co-author, Laura Morton, has made this low-calorie, no-egg version for years. It's the best I have ever had, and we all became immediate converts. You can add as much or as little garlic as you like, and the anchovies are optional.

Serves 4 to 6

8 cups loosely packed, torn, washed, and
  spun-dry romaine lettuce
6 to 8 tablespoons Caesar salad dressing
  (recipe below)
1 cup ½-inch croutons (to make your
  own, see page 111)
¼ cup freshly grated Parmesan cheese,
  optional

In a large bowl, toss together well all the ingredients.

Nutritional Analysis *per serving, including dressing: 127 calories; 67% calories from fat; 10 grams of fat; 224 milligrams of sodium*

CAESAR SALAD DRESSING

Makes about 1 cup

1 heaping tablespoon Dijon mustard
3 garlic cloves, peeled (or more to taste)
5 anchovies or more to taste, soaked in
  water for 15 minutes and drained
  (optional)
4 shakes of Worcestershire sauce (about
  2 teaspoons)
5 shakes of hot sauce, or more to taste
1½ teaspoons black or white pepper
Salt to taste

2 tablespoons fresh lemon juice
2 tablespoons red wine vinegar
½ cup extra-virgin olive oil
¼ cup water

In a blender, puree the first nine ingredients until smooth. With the motor running, add the oil slowly in a stream, and then blend in the water.

Note: This dressing keeps for 1 week, covered and chilled.

CHICKEN WALDORF SALAD

Like Ginger Rogers and Fred Astaire, this combination of ingredients belongs together, which is why I've always loved the taste of a Waldorf salad. All those classic ingredients blend well together naturally, and trust me, the addition of the chicken to this classic is right in step.

Serves 4

¼ cup nonfat plain yogurt
¼ cup low-fat mayonnaise
½ teaspoon honey
Salt and pepper to taste
1 cup chopped apple (such as McIntosh or Red or Golden Delicious), tossed with 2 teaspoons fresh lemon juice
½ cup red grapes, halved
½ cup green grapes, halved
½ cup chopped celery
2 tablespoons chopped scallion
1 skinless, boneless chicken breast (about 12 ounces total), cooked (procedure on page 117) and cubed
1 small cantaloupe, seeds removed and cut into 4 wedges
2 tablespoons chopped walnuts, optional

In a large bowl, whisk together the yogurt, mayonnaise, honey, and salt and pepper to taste. Add the apple, red and green grapes, celery, scallion, and chicken, and toss the mixture well. Mound one-fourth of the salad on top of each wedge of cantaloupe, and top with one-fourth of the walnuts (if using).

Nutritional Analysis *per serving: 251 calories; 27% calories from fat; 8 grams of fat; 164 milligrams of sodium*

CURRIED CHICKEN SALAD
WITH MANGO

I love curry on just about anything you can name. Mango or papaya are the perfect complements, giving this a light and tropical touch.

Serves 4 to 6

4 cups diced, cooked chicken breast (procedure below)
2 tablespoons fresh lime juice
2 mangoes or papayas or a combination of the two, peeled, pitted, and cut into 1-inch pieces
2 celery stalks, chopped
4 scallions, sliced thin (use the white part and some of the green part)
¼ cup nonfat plain yogurt
¼ cup low-fat mayonnaise
1½ teaspoons curry powder
½ teaspoon ground cumin
Salt and pepper to taste
Lettuce for lining the plates
2 tablespoons chopped cashews, optional

In a large bowl, combine the chicken, lime juice, mangoes, celery, and scallions.

In a small bowl, whisk together the yogurt, mayonnaise, spices, and salt and pepper to taste. Add to the chicken mixture, and toss.

Arrange a mound of chicken on top of the lettuce. Garnish each portion with 2 teaspoons of the chopped cashews, if using.

How to poach chicken breasts:
2 boneless, skinless chicken breasts (about 1½ pounds total)
Water or chicken broth to cover

In a saucepan, combine the chicken breast halves with enough water to cover. Remove the chicken from the water and bring the water to a boil. Return the chicken to the pan, and simmer it gently for 5 minutes. Remove the pan from the heat and let it stand, covered, for 10 minutes. Check the chicken to make sure it is cooked through. If it is not, simmer it an additional 2 minutes.

Nutritional Analysis *per serving: 192 calories; 25% calories from fat; 5 grams of fat; 137 milligrams of sodium*

SPINACH SALAD WITH RASPBERRIES AND PAPAYA

My two favorite fruits are raspberries and papayas. We combined the two flavors with a spinach salad to create a colorful, flavorful, vitamin-rich salad. Try adding some chicken to make this a light and healthy main dish.

Serves 4

2 teaspoons grated orange rind
2 tablespoons fresh orange juice
2 tablespoons white wine vinegar
1 teaspoon honey
2 tablespoons canola or vegetable oil
Salt and pepper to taste
10-ounce package fresh spinach, coarse
    stems removed, rinsed and spun dry
1 cup raspberries
1 papaya (or 1 mango, or 2 peaches or
    nectarines), peeled, seeded, and sliced

In a large bowl, whisk together the first five ingredients with salt and pepper to taste. Tear the spinach into bite-size pieces, add it to the dressing along with the raspberries, and toss the salad gently. Arrange one-fourth of the papaya slices on each of four plates, and mound one-fourth of the salad next to the papaya.

Note: If desired, this salad can be made into a main course salad by adding 3 cups cooked and cubed chicken breasts (see procedure on page 117).

Nutritional Analysis *per serving: 130 calories; 46% calories from fat; 7 grams of fat; 59 milligrams of sodium*

SAUTÉED PORTOBELLOS WITH
WARMED FIELD GREENS

My good friend Scot Evans, who loves to cook — especially tasty vegetarian dishes — gave me this recipe. If you've never tasted sautéed or grilled portobellos, run, don't walk, to your grocery store and try them. The large, almost saucer-size brownish mushrooms are meaty in texture and taste out of this world.

Scot Evans

Serves 6

FOR THE DRESSING:
2½ tablespoons balsamic vinegar
1 tablespoon fresh lemon juice
1 tablespoon white wine vinegar
¾ teaspoon sugar
3 tablespoons extra-virgin olive oil
Salt and pepper to taste

FOR THE SALAD:
2 large portobello mushrooms, stems discarded, caps wiped clean with a damp cloth and cut into ¼-inch-thick slices
2 leeks (white and pale green part only), chopped, rinsed well, and patted dry
2 teaspoons extra-virgin olive oil
½ cup Chicken Broth (page 203) or Vegetable Stock (page 204) or canned low-sodium chicken broth
6 cups loosely packed field greens, or a mix of red leaf and Boston lettuce, washed and spun dry

Preheat the oven to 400°F.

Whisk together all the ingredients for the dressing.

Arrange the mushrooms in a shallow roasting pan, sprinkle them with half the dressing, and roast them in the preheated oven for 10 minutes.

In a large skillet, cook the leeks in the oil over moderate heat for 6 minutes or until lightly browned. Add the chicken broth, and boil the mixture until almost all the liquid is evaporated. Add the remaining dressing, and keep the mixture warm.

Mound one-sixth of the greens on each of six plates. Fan out one-sixth of the mushrooms over each mound of greens, and top it with one-sixth of the leek mixture.

Nutritional Analysis *per serving: 123 calories; 61% calories from fat; 9 grams of fat; 74 milligrams of sodium*

CHOPPED VEGETABLE SALAD

For years I've made many versions of this salad, which I vary depending on whether I'm serving my kids or company. For fun, try new combinations of contrasting colored vegetables, chopped into bite-size pieces. The presentation is quite spectacular when you layer the ingredients in a clear glass serving bowl.

Serves 8

1 head of romaine lettuce (or lettuce of choice), rinsed, spun dry, and torn into bite-size pieces (about 6 cups, loosely packed)
1 cup canned kidney beans, drained and rinsed
1 cup canned garbanzo beans, drained and rinsed
1 bunch beets, cooked, peeled, and chopped
3 large carrots, chopped
3 stalks of celery, chopped
3 fresh ears of corn, grilled or boiled and cut off the cob (or 1 cup defrosted frozen corn)
2 medium tomatoes, chopped
2 cups cooked, chopped turkey or poached chicken breast (see procedure on page 117)
1 bunch scallions, chopped
½ cup finely chopped, mixed fresh herbs (e.g., parsley, dill, basil)
½ cup pitted black olives, optional
1½ cups Low-Fat Ranch Dressing (page 124) or your favorite purchased low-fat dressing

Spread the romaine on the bottom of a large glass bowl, and layer the remaining ingredients on top of the lettuce. Add the dressing, and toss well.

Nutritional Analysis *per serving: 217 calories; 25% calories from fat; 6 grams of fat; 357 milligrams of sodium*

CHINESE CHICKEN SALAD

I love the flavor of this Chinese-inspired salad. The dressing is not the least-fattening recipe in my book, but it tastes too good to exclude. It's great for a fun, occasional splurge.

Serves 4

FOR THE DRESSING:

3 tablespoons hoisin sauce
2 tablespoons natural-style peanut butter
2 teaspoons brown sugar
¾ teaspoon Asian chili paste
1 teaspoon freshly grated ginger root
3 tablespoons seasoned rice vinegar
1 tablespoon Asian sesame oil
Salt to taste

FOR THE SALAD:

1 pound skinless, boneless chicken breasts
Nonstick vegetable oil spray
¼ pound dried cappellini
4 cups romaine lettuce, rinsed and spun dry
2 cups shredded carrots
1 bunch scallions, finely chopped (about ¾ cup)
¼ cup chopped coriander

Preheat the oven to 350°F.

Prepare the grill.

In a bowl, whisk together all the ingredients for the dressing.

Spray the chicken lightly with the nonstick vegetable oil spray. Grill the chicken on a rack set 4 inches from the glowing coals for 6 to 8 minutes a side, or until it is just cooked through. Let the chicken stand for 10 minutes before thinly slicing it. (If you prefer, the chicken may be broiled.)

Cook the cappellini according to package instructions, and drain it well. Rinse with cold water, and drain it again. Arrange the pasta in one layer in a large shallow baking pan that has been sprayed with the nonstick vegetable oil spray. Bake the pasta for 20 minutes, or until it is just golden. Season cappellini with salt, if desired, and break it up into ½-inch-length pieces.

In a large bowl, toss the lettuce, carrots, scallions, chicken, cappellini, and coriander with the dressing.

Nutritional Analysis *per serving: 386 calories; 25% calories from fat; 11 grams of fat; 88 milligrams of sodium*

PASTA SALAD WITH SUN-DRIED TOMATOES AND VEGETABLES

Here's a real no-brainer. If you're like me and love pasta in any form, hot or cold, then this recipe will serve you well. Great for dinner hot, it can also be terrific for leftovers the next day cold.

Serves 4 to 6

1 pound dried fusilli, or dried macaroni shells

10-ounce package frozen peas, cooked according to package instructions and drained well

3 ounces sun-dried tomatoes (not oil-packed), rehydrated* and chopped

2 bell peppers (red, yellow, green, or a combination), cut into julienne strips

½ cup plus 2 tablespoons Reduced-Fat Italian Dressing (page 124) or your favorite purchased low-fat or nonfat brand

Salt and pepper to taste

Cook the pasta according to package instructions, rinse with cold water, and drain well.

In a large bowl, combine the pasta with the remaining ingredients. Chill for 1 hour, covered, and serve.

*To rehydrate tomatoes: Pour boiling water over the tomatoes (to cover) and let them stand for 20 minutes. Drain and pat dry.

Nutritional Analysis *per serving: 392 calories; 11% calories from fat; 5 grams of fat; 99 milligrams of sodium*

GLITZY GLADY'S POTATO SALAD

Gladyce Blunden

My mom's famous for her potato salad. Since it was always one of my favorites, I had to include it in my book. I made a few changes from the original, such as cutting back on the number of egg yolks, which reduces the fat without tampering with the flavor. In this age of counting fat grams, if you use too many eggs, the yolk's on you.

Serves 10

3 pounds red potatoes (12 to 14
   medium), scrubbed
Salt and pepper to taste
⅓ cup nonfat plain yogurt
⅓ cup low-fat mayonnaise
2 tablespoons Dijon mustard
2 tablespoons cider or white wine vinegar
4 stalks celery, chopped
3-ounce can sliced, pitted black olives
4-ounce jar sliced pimientos, drained and
   rinsed
2 hard-boiled eggs plus the whites of 2
   more eggs, chopped
2 tablespoons chopped scallions
3 tablespoons chopped fresh parsley
Paprika for sprinkling

Place the potatoes in a saucepan with water to cover. Season with salt, bring to a boil, and simmer for 20 to 25 minutes, or just until tender. Drain, and let them cool until they can be handled. Cut into bite-size pieces.

In a large bowl, whisk together the yogurt, mayonnaise, mustard, vinegar, and salt and pepper to taste. Add the potatoes and all the remaining ingredients except the paprika, and toss well. Sprinkle liberally with the paprika.

Nutritional Analysis *per serving: 184 calories; 23% calories
from fat; 5 grams of fat; 266 milligrams of sodium*

SALAD DRESSINGS

The following are some easy and delicious recipes that you can make and keep in your refrigerator ahead of time. Homemade salad dressings are a treat, and add a special flavor to any salad.

REDUCED-FAT ITALIAN DRESSING

Makes 1 cup

½ cup balsamic vinegar
¼ cup red wine vinegar
2 garlic cloves, minced (about 2 teaspoons), or to taste
¼ teaspoon dried oregano
¼ teaspoon dried basil
Salt and pepper to taste
2 tablespoons olive oil
2 tablespoons Chicken Broth (page 203) or canned reduced-sodium chicken broth

In a bowl, whisk together the first five ingredients. Whisk in the oil and the chicken broth.

Nutritional Analysis *per 1-tablespoon serving: 23 calories; 63% calories from fat; 2 grams of fat; 7 milligrams of sodium*

LOW-FAT RANCH DRESSING

Makes about 1 cup

¾ cup buttermilk
¼ cup low-fat mayonnaise
2 tablespoons white wine vinegar
1 tablespoon minced fresh parsley
1 tablespoon minced fresh chives or scallion greens
½ to 1 garlic clove (about ½ to 1 teaspoon), minced, or to taste
½ to 1 teaspoon onion powder or to taste
Salt and pepper to taste

In a bowl, whisk together all the ingredients.

Nutritional Analysis *per 1-tablespoon serving: 20 calories; 64% calories from fat; 1 gram of fat; 36 milligrams of sodium*

LOW-FAT HONEY MUSTARD DRESSING

Makes about 1 cup

¼ cup low-fat mayonnaise
¼ cup Dijon mustard
2 tablespoons honey
½ cup distilled white vinegar
Salt and pepper to taste

In a bowl, whisk together the mayonnaise, mustard, and honey until smooth. Stir in the vinegar, and add salt and pepper to taste.

Nutritional Analysis *per 1-tablespoon serving: 21 calories; 23% calories from fat; ½ gram of fat; 169 milligrams of sodium*

GMA family shot

Chapter 9

PASTAS, GRAINS, AND RICE

SPENCER CHRISTIAN'S PASTA WITH TURKEY MEATBALLS

Spencer Christian

Since *Good Morning America*'s Spencer Christian was inspirational and instrumental in my weight loss and conversion to healthier eating, I had to include a couple of his recipes in my book. This pasta and meatball recipe shows that often a fat-laden recipe can be made deliciously more healthful. Spencer uses ground turkey breast in place of ground beef. A serving gives you only 6 grams of fat, which is low for a hearty entree.

Serves 4 to 6

1 pound ground, raw turkey (preferably breast meat)
⅓ cup seasoned bread crumbs
¼ cup water
¼ teaspoon salt, optional
Pepper to taste
Nonstick vegetable oil spray
3 cups Roasted Fresh Tomato Sauce (page 197) or your favorite purchased tomato sauce
1 pound dried linguine or spaghetti

Preheat the oven to 350°F.

In a bowl, combine well the turkey, bread crumbs, water, salt (if using), and pepper to taste.

To check the seasoning: Take 1 tablespoon of the mixture and cook it in a small skillet sprayed with the nonstick vegetable oil spray. Taste and correct the seasoning if necessary.

Roll the mixture into meatballs the size of walnuts. Arrange the meatballs in one layer in a shallow roasting pan sprayed with the nonstick vegetable oil spray and bake them for 20 minutes, or until they are cooked through.

In a saucepan, heat the tomato sauce over moderate heat until it is hot, add the meatballs, and stir the mixture gently.

Cook the linguine according to package instructions, and drain well. Divide the pasta among four bowls. Top each portion with one-fourth of the meatballs and tomato sauce.

Nutritional Analysis *per serving: 436 calories; 12% calories from fat; 6 grams of fat; 89 milligrams of sodium*

SPENCER CHRISTIAN'S SPAGHETTI WITH LENTIL SAUCE

Serves 4 to 6

½ cup dried lentils, picked over and
  rinsed
1 medium onion, chopped (about 1 cup)
2 garlic cloves, minced (about 2 teaspoons)
2 teaspoons olive oil
3¾ cups Roasted Fresh Tomato Sauce
  (page 197) or two 15-ounce cans of
  your favorite purchased tomato sauce
1 cup seeded and chopped tomato
2 cups water
½ teaspoon dried oregano
½ teaspoon dried basil
½ teaspoon dried thyme
¼ teaspoon salt, optional
2 dashes hot sauce
1 pound dried spaghetti

In a saucepan simmer the lentils in water for 30 to 45 minutes, or until they are tender, and drain well. In a large skillet, cook the onion and the garlic in the oil over moderately low heat until the onion is softened. Add the tomato sauce, chopped tomato, water, spices, salt (if using), hot sauce, and cooked lentils. Simmer the mixture until it is heated through. Cook the spaghetti according to packages instructions and drain well. Top each portion with some of the lentil sauce.

Nutritional Analysis *per serving: 444 calories; 15% calories from fat; 8 grams of fat; 212 milligrams of sodium*

SPENCER CHRISTIAN'S
TURKEY LASAGNA

Lasagna is often so heavy with meat and cheese that after you eat it, rectangular servings can clearly be detected under stirrup stretch pants. Would I lie? Spencer saves us all from ourselves with his reduced-fat version.

Serves 8

6 ounces ground, raw turkey
2 medium onions, chopped (about 2 cups)
1 carrot, chopped
½ tablespoon olive oil
¾ pound shiitake mushrooms, stems discarded, caps wiped clean and chopped
2 garlic cloves, chopped (about 2 teaspoons)
Salt and pepper to taste
¼ cup dry red wine
28-ounce can crushed tomatoes
½ cup sun-dried tomatoes (not oil-packed), rehydrated* and cut into slivers with kitchen shears
1¼ cups water
½ teaspoon dried oregano
½ teaspoon dried basil
¼ teaspoon dried thyme
Red pepper flakes to taste
12 dried lasagna noodles (about 12 ounces)
Nonstick vegetable oil spray
1-pound container of 1% cottage cheese, pureed in a food processor or blender until smooth
8 ounces part-skim mozzarella cheese, coarsely grated
½ cup freshly grated Parmesan cheese (about 1½ ounces)
2 tablespoons chopped fresh parsley

Preheat the oven to 350°F.

In a large nonstick skillet, cook the turkey over moderately high heat, breaking up the meat with a wooden spoon, for 3 to 5 minutes or until it is no longer pink. Transfer it to a colander to drain and set it aside.

In a large, heavy saucepan or Dutch oven (preferably nonstick), cook the onions and the carrot in the oil over moderate heat for 2 to 3 minutes or until softened. Add the mushrooms, garlic, and salt and pepper to taste and cook, stirring frequently, for 3 minutes or until the shiitakes are tender. Add the wine, crushed tomatoes, sun-dried tomatoes, water, herbs, red pepper flakes, and the reserved turkey and bring the mixture to a simmer. Cook, covered, over low heat, stirring occasionally, for 2 hours. Add a little water if the sauce becomes too dry. Taste and adjust seasoning.

Cook the lasagna noodles according to package instructions, drain, and cool by plunging into a large bowl of ice-cold water. Lay the noodles out on kitchen towels.

Spray a 13×9-inch baking dish with the nonstick spray. Spread about 1 cup of the meat sauce in the bottom of the prepared pan. Lay 3 noodles on top. Spread another cup of meat sauce over the noodles, and top it with about ½ cup of the cottage cheese. Sprinkle ½ cup of the mozzarella and 2 tablespoons of the Parmesan over the cottage cheese and repeat the whole procedure to make another 3 layers, finishing with sauce and cheese. Sprinkle with the parsley and bake for 35 to 40 minutes or until the sauce is bubbling. Remove from the oven and let the lasagna set for 5 to 10 minutes before cutting.

To rehydrate tomatoes: Pour boiling water over the tomatoes (to cover) and let them stand for 20 minutes. Drain and pat dry.

Nutritional Analysis *per serving: 383 calories; 19% calories from fat; 8 grams of fat; 616 milligrams of sodium*

BROCCOLI PASTA

I first tasted this pasta at a dinner party at the home of my co-author, Laura Morton. I absolutely refused to believe it was not fattening. Fortunately, not only is it healthful, it's incredibly quick and easy to make. That's right up my cooking alley.

Serves 4 to 6

1 head broccoli, the stalk peeled and cut into ½-inch lengths, the top cut into small florets
3 cups Chicken Broth (page 203) or canned reduced-sodium chicken broth
4 dashes hot sauce
4 garlic cloves, minced (1 heaping tablespoon)
½ medium onion, chopped (about ½ cup), optional
1 cup sliced mushrooms, optional
1 pound dried cappellini or dried spaghettini
¼ cup freshly grated Parmesan cheese
Freshly ground black pepper to taste

In a large pot of boiling water, blanch the broccoli for 3 to 5 minutes or until it is crisp tender, and drain well.

In a large saucepan, bring the chicken broth to a boil, add the hot sauce, garlic, onions, and mushrooms (if using), and simmer for 10 minutes.

In another large pot of boiling water, cook the cappellini according to package instructions and drain it. Add the broccoli to the broth to heat it. Divide the cappellini among 4 bowls, pour one-fourth of the broccoli broth mixture over each one and top with the Parmesan and freshly ground black pepper to taste.

Nutritional Analysis *per serving: 334 calories; 10% calories from fat; 4 grams of fat; 451 milligrams of sodium*

TOMATO AND FRESH BASIL PASTA

This is a classic example of simple being best. Fresh tomatoes at the peak of the season from the garden or farmer's market are made into a sauce that's cooked briefly. Toss it with penne pasta and fresh basil, and top it off with a dusting of fresh Parmesan. You may never want to go back to marinara.

Serves 4 to 6

16 plum tomatoes
6 to 8 garlic cloves, minced (about 6 to 8
    teaspoons), or to taste
1 tablespoon olive oil
1 cup Chicken Broth (page 203), canned
    reduced-sodium chicken broth, Veg-
    etable Stock (page 204), or water
½ pound dried penne
½ cup chopped fresh basil
6 tablespoons grated fresh Parmesan

Drop the tomatoes into a pot of boiling water for 30 seconds to 1 minute or until their skins start to slip off, and transfer them to a bowl of ice and water.

Peel the tomatoes, remove the seeds, and coarsely chop them.

In a large nonstick skillet, cook the garlic in the oil over moderately low heat for 8 minutes, or until it is golden. Add the tomatoes and the broth, bring the mixture to a boil, and simmer for 20 to 30 minutes, or until the liquid has reduced by half. Keep the sauce warm.

Cook the penne according to package instructions and drain it well.

Add the basil and salt and pepper to taste to the sauce. Spoon the sauce over the pasta and sprinkle some of the Parmesan over each portion.

Nutritional Analysis *per serving: 361 calories; 15% calories from fat; 6 grams of fat; 248 milligrams of sodium*

BARBARA BRANDT'S FITNESS FETTUCCINE

It's only proper that my personal fitness trainer whips up this delicious Fitness Fettuccine. Leave it to Barbara to develop a recipe that wouldn't negate all her hard work and discipline as a trainer.

Serves 4 to 6

1 pound thin asparagus (about 1 bunch), the tough ends removed and the stalks peeled
Nonstick vegetable oil spray
1 teaspoon extra-virgin olive oil
½ pound fresh shiitake mushrooms, stems discarded, caps wiped clean and sliced
2 garlic cloves, minced (about 2 teaspoons)
3 tablespoons chopped fresh parsley
2 tablespoons chopped fresh basil
¼ cup sun-dried tomatoes (not oil-packed), rehydrated* and chopped
1 cup dry white wine
1 cup Chicken Broth (page 203) or canned reduced-sodium chicken broth
1 pound dried fettuccine
2 tablespoons pine nuts
½ cup freshly grated Parmesan
Salt and pepper to taste

Cut the asparagus into ½-inch diagonal slices. Spray a large nonstick pan with the nonstick vegetable oil spray, add the olive oil, and heat over moderately high heat until hot. Add the asparagus and sauté for 1 minute. Add the mushrooms and garlic and sauté for 5 minutes. Add the herbs, tomatoes, wine, and broth and simmer for 6 minutes.

Cook the fettuccine according to package instructions, drain well, and transfer to a large bowl. Add the pasta sauce, pine nuts, Parmesan, and salt and pepper to taste and toss well.

*To rehydrate tomatoes: Pour boiling water over the tomatoes (to cover) and let them stand for 20 minutes. Drain and pat dry.

Nutritional Analysis *per serving: 393 calories; 15% calories from fat; 7 grams of fat; 291 milligrams of sodium*

STEVEN RAICHLEN'S SPAGHETTI WITH WHITE BEAN SAUCE

Steven Raichlen

My co-host, Charlie Gibson, doesn't go for so-called meatless main dishes. But he really liked this one when creative cookbook author Steven Raichlen made it for us on *GMA*. Steven has cooked up some of the most flavorful low-fat dishes ever on our show. My daughter Jamie loved it, and she's my personal authority on vegetarian cooking. Combining rice or pasta with beans gives you a complete source of protein.

Serves 4 to 6

4 garlic cloves, minced (about 4 teaspoons)
2 red onions, finely chopped
1 red bell pepper, cut into ¼-inch dice
6 celery stalks, cut into ¼-inch dice
2 tablespoons olive oil
2 cups cooked (or canned) navy or Great Northern beans, drained and rinsed
2 cups Vegetable Stock (page 204), Chicken Broth (page 203), or canned low-sodium chicken broth
½ cup finely chopped flat-leaf parsley
¼ to ½ teaspoon red pepper flakes, or to taste, optional
1 pound dried spaghetti
2 to 4 ounces freshly grated Parmesan, optional

In a large nonstick skillet, cook the garlic, onion, pepper, and celery in the oil over moderately low heat for 5 minutes or until softened.

Stir in the beans and cook for 1 minute. Add the stock, half the parsley, pepper flakes (if using), and salt and pepper to taste. Simmer for 5 minutes.

Coarsely mash half the beans with a fork.

Cook the spaghetti according to package instructions and drain well. In a large bowl, toss together the spaghetti and the bean sauce. Sprinkle with the remaining parsley and serve at once with the Parmesan, if using.

Nutritional Analysis *per serving: 488 calories; 21% calories from fat; 11 grams of fat; 540 milligrams of sodium*

CREAMY PASTA WITH VEGETABLES

Just the word *creamy* could sell me on this recipe. But get this: There's no cream in it at all! See if you don't agree that this recipe satisfies your craving for cream sauce and still lets you fit into your favorite jeans.

Serves 4

½ pound dried linguine or dried
   spaghetti or dried pasta of choice
2 carrots, sliced thin
2 ounces snow peas or 1 cup defrosted
   frozen peas
½ red bell pepper, sliced thin
1½ tablespoons vegetable oil or butter
4 mushrooms, sliced thin
1 garlic clove, minced (about 1 teaspoon),
   optional
2 tablespoons all-purpose flour
1¾ cups Chicken Broth (page 203) or
   canned reduced-sodium chicken broth,
   heated
½ cup 1% milk
3 tablespoons freshly grated Parmesan
2 tablespoons chopped fresh herbs (e.g.,
   basil, chives, dill, parsley)
Salt and pepper to taste

Cook the pasta according to package instructions and drain well.

While the pasta is cooking, drop the carrots and snow peas into boiling water for 30 seconds, drain, and set aside. In a large nonstick skillet, cook the pepper in the oil over moderate heat for 5 minutes. Add the mushrooms and the garlic, if using, and cook for 5 minutes. Sprinkle the flour over the vegetables and cook the mixture for 2 minutes. Whisk in the broth in a steady stream, bring the mixture back to a boil, and stir in the milk, cheese, carrots, snow peas, herbs, and drained, cooked pasta. Add salt and pepper to taste and heat through.

Note: Other vegetables can be added to this dish: blanched broccoli florets, blanched cauliflower florets, corn, or sliced zucchini.

Nutritional Analysis *per serving: 318 calories; 23% calories
from fat; 8 grams of fat; 261 milligrams of sodium*

TERRA'S PAGLIA E FIENO

From one of my favorite restaurants in Greenwich, Connecticut, this one's guaranteed to please your eyes with its colorful contrasts, and your palate with its interesting combination of textures and flavors.

Serves 4 to 6

9-ounce package fresh egg linguine
9-ounce package fresh spinach linguine
3 garlic cloves, sliced
3 tablespoons extra-virgin olive oil
8 anchovy fillets, soaked in water for 10
    minutes, drained, and patted dry
4 tablespoons capers
24 Kalamata olives, pitted, optional
3 ounces sun-dried tomatoes (not oil-
    packed), rehydrated* and cut into
    julienne strips
20 large shrimp (16–20 size), peeled and
    deveined
¼ cup dry white wine
¾ cup Vegetable Stock (page 204), shrimp
    stock,† or Chicken Broth (page 203)
15 basil leaves, shredded
2 tablespoons chopped parsley
Salt and pepper to taste

Cook the linguine according to package directions and drain well.

In a large nonstick skillet, cook the garlic in the oil over moderately high heat for about 6 minutes, or until it is light brown. Add the anchovies and cook the mixture for 1 minute. Stir in the capers, olives, sun-dried tomatoes, and shrimp, and cook for 3 minutes. Add the wine and simmer until almost all of it is evaporated. Add the stock, basil, and parsley and simmer for 3 more minutes or until the shrimp are just cooked through. Add salt and pepper to taste and serve the sauce over the linguine.

*To rehydrate sun-dried tomatoes: Pour boiling water over the tomatoes (to cover) and let them stand for 20 minutes. Drain and pat dry.
†To make shrimp stock: Add the shells from the shrimp to vegetable stock or chicken broth, and simmer for 20 minutes.

Nutritional Analysis *per serving: 460 calories; 23% calories from fat; 11 grams of fat; 677 milligrams of sodium*

P O L E N T A

I absolutely love polenta. If you've never cooked it, you might assume it's demanding or tricky to make. But, basically, it's uncomplicated — and rather humble. Cornmeal is blended with a home-made (especially if you want to slash that sodium figure) or canned broth and some simple season-ings. My kids like polenta all by itself, but I like to use different toppings, such as roasted vegetables or sautéed mushrooms, when I'm serving this to friends.

Serves 6

4 cups Vegetable Stock (page 204), or
*   Chicken Broth (page 203), or canned*
*   reduced-sodium chicken broth*
3 cups water
2 cups yellow cornmeal
Salt and pepper to taste

OPTIONAL ADDITIONS:
¼ cup freshly grated Parmesan cheese
3 tablespoons chopped fresh herbs (such as
*   parsley, thyme, rosemary, chives, basil)*
2 garlic cloves, minced (about 2 tea-
*   spoons), sautéed in 2 teaspoons olive*
*   oil over low heat until soft*
1 recipe Mushroom Topping (page 80)
1 recipe Roasted Vegetables (page 193)

In a saucepan bring the broth and water to a boil. Add the cornmeal in a slow even stream, whisking, until all the cornmeal has been added. Turn down the heat to low and cook, stirring very frequently, for 20 to 25 minutes or until the polenta starts to pull away from the sides of the pan as you stir. Add salt and pepper to taste and any of the optional ingre-dients, if desired.

Nutritional Analysis *per serving, without optional additions:*
160 calories; 11% calories from fat; 2 grams of fat; 422
milligrams of sodium

QUICK AND EASY PAELLA

When I studied in Mexico, I lived on paella for breakfast, lunch, and dinner. My roommates and I would cook up large vats of it so that we could dine on it all week. This was adapted from well-known cookbook author Patsy Jamieson's recipe, with a few ingredients added just for fun.

Serves 4 to 6

3 teaspoons olive oil
½ pound medium shrimp, peeled and deveined
½ pound sea scallops
½ pound boneless, skinless chicken breast,
   cut into ½-inch pieces
1 medium onion, chopped (about 1 cup)
2 to 3 garlic cloves, minced (2 to 3 teaspoons), or to taste
14½-ounce can tomatoes, chopped, juice
   reserved
½ teaspoon saffron
½ teaspoon paprika
2 dashes hot sauce or to taste
1 cup medium grain white rice, preferably arborio
2 cups Chicken Broth (page 203) or
   canned low-sodium chicken broth
4-ounce jar sliced pimientos, drained and
   rinsed
1 cup defrosted frozen peas or corn
Salt and pepper to taste

In a large nonstick skillet, heat 1 teaspoon of the oil over moderately high heat. Add the shrimp and sauté for 3 to 4 minutes or until they turn pink.

Transfer the shrimp with a slotted spoon to a bowl, and add another teaspoon of the oil to the skillet. Sauté the scallops in the oil for 3 to 4 minutes or until they are very lightly browned. Transfer the scallops with the slotted spoon to the bowl. Add the remaining oil to the pan, sauté the chicken for 4 minutes, and transfer it to the bowl.

Add the onion and the garlic to the pan, and cook the mixture over low heat for 6 minutes or until the onion is lightly colored. Stir in the tomatoes, saffron, paprika, and hot sauce, and simmer for 3 minutes. Add the rice and stir to coat well. Stir in the broth and bring to a boil. Cover tightly and simmer over low heat for 20 minutes. Add the shrimp, scallops, chicken, pimientos, and peas; cover and cook the paella, stirring occasionally for 5 to 10 minutes more, or until the rice is tender. Season with salt and pepper to taste.

Nutritional Analysis per serving: 331 calories; 14% calories from fat; 5 grams of fat; 581 milligrams of sodium

QUICK RISOTTO

If I had to pick a favorite single food that comforts me the most, it would probably be rice, especially when made into risotto. For years, I thought risotto was too hard to make. But this recipe proved me wrong. It's easy, quick, and delicious. Our optional additions add color and flavor, but few calories.

Serves 4 to 6

5 to 6 cups Vegetable Stock (page 204), or
  Chicken Broth (page 203), or canned
  reduced-sodium chicken broth, heated
½ medium onion, chopped (about ½ cup)
1 tablespoon olive or vegetable oil
1½ cups arborio rice (uncooked)
⅓ cup dry white wine
2 tablespoons freshly grated Parmesan
Salt and pepper to taste

OPTIONAL ADDITIONS:
2 ounces cultivated or wild mushrooms
  (caps wiped clean with a damp cloth,
  and sliced)
½ cup defrosted frozen peas
½ cup blanched broccoli florets
6 stalks asparagus, cooked and chopped

Bring the stock to a boil in a saucepan and keep it at a gentle simmer.

In a large heavy saucepan, cook the onion in the oil over moderately low heat for 5 minutes or until it is softened. (If using the optional mushrooms or red pepper, add them at this point and cook the mixture for an additional 5 minutes.) Add the rice and stir it to coat all the grains well with the onion mixture. Add the wine and bring to a boil, stirring constantly. When most of the wine is absorbed, stir in ½ cup of the broth. Simmer the rice, stirring constantly, until most of the liquid is absorbed. Continue cooking and adding broth, ½ cup at a time, stirring constantly and letting each portion be absorbed before adding the next. After the last broth addition, the rice should still be chewy and creamy.) This whole process should take about 25 minutes.

Stir in the Parmesan and the salt and pepper to taste (and any of the optional ingredients, if using).

Nutritional Analysis *per serving, without optional additions: 239 calories; 16% calories from fat; 4 grams of fat; 676 milligrams of sodium*

HERBED COUSCOUS WITH LEMON

Couscous is technically a pasta, but it's even quicker than most pastas or rice. This is a super-quick, easy, lemony side dish. Couscous saved my life . . . really, I'm not kidding. I've been to Morocco twice now, and I would have starved to death if it weren't for couscous. I serve couscous with chicken, meat, and fish. It really complements almost anything, and is a nice change from rice.

Serves 4

1½ cups Chicken Broth (page 203),
    canned reduced-sodium chicken broth,
    or water
½ teaspoon freshly grated lemon zest
1 cup couscous
2 tablespoons chopped fresh parsley
    leaves, or fresh dill or fresh basil (or 2
    teaspoons dried thyme or oregano)
1 tablespoon extra-virgin olive oil
Fresh lemon juice to taste
Salt and pepper to taste

In a small, heavy saucepan, bring the chicken broth to a boil, stir in the zest and the couscous, and remove the pan from the heat. Let the mixture stand, covered, for 5 minutes. Then fluff it with a fork, and stir in the parsley, the olive oil, the lemon juice, and salt and pepper to taste. Serve with Jewel of the Nile Chicken Kebabs (page 154).

Nutritional Analysis *per serving: 212 calories; 18% calories from fat; 4 grams of fat; 265 milligrams of sodium*

Chapter 10

MEAT AND POULTRY

JOIE'S LAMB SHISH KEBABS

Grandma Joie pulls through again, this time with a kebab recipe — and for those of you on the run, notice the quick salad dressing version. You'll be surprised at how great these easy kebabs taste.

Serves 4

FOR THE MARINADE:

3 tablespoons vegetable oil
2 tablespoons fresh lemon juice
2 tablespoons grated onion
2 teaspoons grated fresh ginger
1 garlic clove, minced (about 1 teaspoon)
1 teaspoon ground turmeric
1 teaspoon ground coriander
1 teaspoon ground cumin
A good pinch cayenne

FOR THE KEBABS:

1½ pounds lean lamb cut into 1-inch
   cubes
2 green peppers, cut into 1-inch pieces
2 onions, cut into 1-inch-thick wedges
16 ripe cherry tomatoes, or 2 ripe toma-
   toes cut into eighths
Salt and pepper to taste

Make the marinade by combining all the ingredients in a bowl and stirring well. Add the lamb, the peppers, and the onions and toss well to coat. Let the mixture marinate for 1 hour.

Prepare the grill.

Arrange the meat, onions, peppers, and tomatoes alternately on 4 large skewers or 8 small skewers. Brush some of the marinade left in the bottom of the bowl on the tomatoes. Arrange the skewers on a prepared grill, 4 inches from the glowing coals. Cook, turning several times, for about 10 minutes for medium-rare lamb. (Alternatively, broil the skewers set on a rack 4 inches from a preheated broiler.)

If time is a factor: In a bowl, cover the lamb, onions, and peppers with 1 cup Reduced-Fat Italian Dressing (page 124) and marinate in refrigerator overnight so the ingredients will be ready to skewer and cook the next day.

Nutritional Analysis *per serving: 265 calories; 31% calories from fat; 9 grams of fat; 89 milligrams of sodium*

IRENE'S ROASTED LEG OF LAMB

This is an old Greek recipe, passed down from generation to generation — but not in my family. It's a favorite of Irene Katris, who was my bookkeeper for a number of years. While it's not the skinniest recipe in this book, it's worthy of an occasional splurge, and well worth the time and tender loving care that it takes to produce. Serve the usual mint jelly with this slow-cooked, fall-off-the-bone leg of lamb. A 6-pound leg of lamb is enough for sixteen servings, so this is an ideal recipe for a small dinner party.

Serves 16

6-pound leg of lamb, trimmed of all visible fat
4 to 8 garlic cloves or to taste, sliced
2 tablespoons extra-virgin olive oil
2 tablespoons dried oregano
Salt and pepper to taste
Juice of 2 lemons
2 onions, chopped coarse
3 carrots, chopped coarse
2½ pounds small red potatoes, scrubbed
2 zucchini, chopped coarse
Paprika to taste

Preheat the oven to 500°F.

Using the tip of a knife, cut small slits all over the lamb. Wedge the garlic slices into the slits (using as much of the garlic as you like). Rub the lamb all over with the olive oil, the oregano, and salt and pepper to taste. Put the lamb in a large roasting pan, and squeeze the lemons over it. Arrange all the vegetables around the lamb and season them to taste with the paprika. Add ¼ inch of water to the pan, and roast the lamb and vegetables in the preheated oven for 30 minutes. Turn the oven down to 300°F., and roast the lamb for 2½ to 3 more hours (or until a meat thermometer registers 160°F.), basting it with the juices from time to time and adding additional water if necessary. (The lamb must be well cooked to develop the right flavor.) Let the lamb rest for 20 minutes before carving. Serve each portion with some of the vegetables.

Nutritional Analysis *per serving: 300 calories; 28% calories from fat; 9 grams of fat; 78 milligrams of sodium*

MOM'S POT ROAST

Another favorite for occasional enjoyment. But this homey favorite will never be scratched from my life forever, simply savored now and then. Whenever I remember my childhood days, I am reminded of walking into my mom's house and smelling the delicious aroma of her pot roast. It was so tender that we always called it "tear-apart meat." This recipe can be made ahead of time and refrigerated. Excess fat can be easily removed when it is chilled, and that reduces the fat content considerably. My mom's pot roast tastes even better the next day!

Joan and her mom

Serves 14

2 tablespoons olive or vegetable oil
4 pounds rump roast, trimmed of all fat
Salt and pepper to taste
1 large onion, cut into eighths
2 cups water or 1½ cups water and ½
    cup dry red wine
1 cup Chicken Broth (page 203) or
    canned low-sodium chicken broth
2 tablespoons Worcestershire sauce
2 bay leaves
2 baking potatoes (about 1¼ to 1½
    pounds total), peeled and cut into
    1-inch pieces
6 carrots, cut into 1-inch lengths
¼ cup Wondra flour

In a Dutch oven, heat the oil over moderately high heat. Add the roast, seasoned with salt and pepper to taste, and brown it on all sides. Add the onion and cook for 5 minutes or until it is lightly browned. Add the water (and wine, if using), broth, Worcestershire sauce, and bay leaves. Bring the mixture to a boil, and simmer, covered tightly, for 2 hours. Check from time to time to make sure the water has not reduced too much, and add more as necessary. Add the potatoes and the carrots and simmer, covered, for 30 minutes more or until both the vegetables and the meat are very tender. Strain the liquid, and skim off the fat and discard it.* Measure the liquid. If there is more than 2½ cups, simmer the liquid until it is reduced to 2½ cups. If there is less, add enough water to measure 2½ cups. In a small bowl, whisk together ½ cup of water with the flour, and whisk the mixture slowly into the liquid. Bring the liquid to a boil, and simmer it for 5 minutes. Add salt and pepper to taste, and pour the sauce over the meat and the vegetables.

The fat is much easier to remove if the pot roast is prepared a day ahead up to this point, and refrigerated overnight. The fat will rise to the top and solidify. Scoop off and discard the fat. Return the Dutch oven to the stove, bring the liquid to a boil, and simmer, covered, until the pot roast is heated through.

    Proceed with the rest of the recipe. The pot roast actually improves in flavor if made a day ahead.

Nutritional Analysis *per serving: 275 calories; 30% calories from fat; 9 grams of fat; 132 milligrams of sodium*

GRANDMA JOIE'S BEEF BRISKET

How could I possibly write a cookbook — even a healthful one — without sharing some of my favorite recipes, such as Grandma Joie's Beef Brisket? Brisket's never been known for its leanness. But if I skipped such gems, you wouldn't forgive me, and neither would Grandma Joie, my former mother-in-law. So a few higher-calorie, fat and/or sodium recipes are included in this collection, for occasional dietary splurges. Yes, we could have dropped the nutritional numbers for them, but that would be cheating. And eating well means being honest with yourself about how and what you eat most of the time.

Serves 14

4 pounds first cut of beef brisket
3 tablespoons minced garlic
4 cups sliced onions
2 cups Chicken Broth (page 203) or
    canned reduced-sodium chicken broth
2 cups water
1½ cups Tomato Sauce (pages 197–98) or
    a 12-ounce jar chili sauce
2 pounds small red potatoes, or a
    1-pound package frozen lima beans

Preheat the oven to 350°F.

Season the brisket all over with salt and pepper, and rub it with the garlic. In a large roasting pan, combine the onions, the broth, and the water, and add the brisket. Spread the tomato sauce over the top of it and add the potatoes (or lima beans) to the pan. Put the pan on top of 1 or 2 burners (however it will fit) and bring the broth to a boil over high heat. Cover the pan tightly and cook the brisket in the oven for 3½ to 4 hours or until the meat is fork tender. Add additional water if the liquid gets too low during the cooking process. Strain the liquid, and skim off and discard the fat.

Nutritional Analysis *per serving: 295 calories; 39% calories from fat; 13 grams of fat; 347 milligrams of sodium*

EASY STUFFED CABBAGE

I never knew that I liked stuffed cabbage until I tried Grandma Joie's. Once I did, I was hooked forever — and had to know how to make it. At first, she offered her traditional family recipe that takes all day to prepare and requires constant testing to achieve the right balance between sweet and sour. When I reported back that it was a hit, but it was too much of a pain to make, she confessed there was indeed a shortcut version. It tasted the same to me; I'm sharing it, and hope you'll agree.

Makes 8 rolls

1 cabbage (about 2 to 2¼ pounds), tough outer leaves and core removed
1 pound lean ground beef
½ cup cooked white rice
1 large egg, beaten lightly
Salt to taste
½ teaspoon freshly ground pepper
One 14-ounce can sauerkraut, drained
1-liter bottle ginger ale
1½ cups Roasted Fresh Tomato Sauce (page 197), or a 12-ounce bottle chili sauce

Preheat the oven to 350°F.

In a saucepan cover the cabbage with water, bring to a boil, and cook for 3 minutes. Drain, and run cold water over the cabbage until it is cold enough to handle. Remove 8 large outer leaves, cut out and discard 1 to 2 inches of the tough rib on each leaf, and pat the leaves dry.

Chop the remaining cabbage. In a bowl, combine the beef, rice, egg, salt to taste, and the pepper. Roll up one-eighth of the beef mixture in each cabbage leaf.

In the bottom of a lasagna or roasting pan, spread one-half of the shredded cabbage, and top it with one-half of the sauerkraut. Arrange the cabbage rolls, seam side down, on top of the sauerkraut, and top them with the remaining shredded cabbage and sauerkraut.

In a large bowl, whisk together the ginger ale and the tomato sauce, and pour the mixture over the rolls. Put the pan on top of the burners, and bring the liquid to a boil. Cover the pan tightly with foil, and bake it for 2 hours in the preheated oven.

Nutritional Analysis *per serving: 264 calories; 32% calories from fat; 10 grams of fat; 323 milligrams of sodium*

BEEF AND BROCCOLI STIR-FRY

I like to wok on the wild side . . . cooking stir-fry is a lot of fun for the whole family. There are as many variations as you can think of. Be creative! Serve over rice — one of my favorites — and try eating with chopsticks.

Serves 4

2 tablespoons reduced-sodium soy sauce
2½ teaspoons brown sugar
2 teaspoons cornstarch
4½ teaspoons vegetable oil
1 pound beef tenderloin, cut into rectangles about ¼ inch thick and 1 inch long*
Florets from 1 head of broccoli
4 mushrooms, wiped clean with a damp cloth and sliced
1 garlic clove, minced (about 1 teaspoon)
2 teaspoons minced or finely grated fresh ginger root
1½ tablespoons dry sherry
2 ounces snow peas, blanched in boiling water for 30 seconds and drained
½ cup sliced water chestnuts

In a bowl, whisk together 1 tablespoon of the soy sauce, ½ teaspoon of the sugar, the cornstarch, and 1½ teaspoons of the vegetable oil. Add the beef and toss it well to coat each piece. Chill, covered, for at least 30 minutes and up to 8 hours.

In a large nonstick pan, heat 1 teaspoon of the remaining oil over high heat until it is just smoking. Add the beef and stir-fry for 1 minute or until browned on all sides. Remove the beef from the pan with tongs, and add the remaining oil to the pan. When the pan is hot again, add the broccoli and stir-fry for 1 to 2 minutes or until golden. Add the mushrooms and stir-fry for 1 minute. Add the garlic and ginger, and cook for 30 seconds. Add the sherry, the remaining soy sauce and brown sugar, snow peas and water chestnuts, and cook for 1 minute or until heated through.

Note: Other vegetables can be used in this dish: sliced carrots, blanched cauliflower, strips of red, green, and yellow peppers, or sliced parsnips.

*The beef is easier to slice if placed in the freezer for 30 minutes.

Nutritional Analysis *per serving: 395 calories; 29% calories from fat; 13 grams of fat; 366 milligrams of sodium*

ACADEMY AWARD—WINNING CHILI BURGERS

Patsy Jamieson, test kitchen director for *Eating Well* magazine, appeared on *GMA* the day of the 1995 Academy Awards. She prepared five dishes that reflected the 1994 movies nominated for best picture. Her Chili Burgers, in honor of *Pulp Fiction,* are neither pulpy nor fictitious. It's tough work, but I was the judge and had to pick my favorite. It was a one-woman sweep for the Chili Burgers, so much so that I have included them for you to try at home.

Joan and Patsy Jamieson

Serves 4

1 slice firm white bread, torn into small pieces
2 tablespoons tomato paste
2 tablespoons water
¾ pound ground raw turkey, or lean ground beef
⅔ cup canned black beans, drained, rinsed, and coarsely chopped
2 tablespoons chopped fresh coriander or parsley
1 teaspoon dried thyme
Salt to taste
½ teaspoon freshly ground black pepper
1 teaspoon canola or vegetable oil
1 small onion, chopped fine (about ½ cup)
1 garlic clove, minced (about 1 teaspoon)
1 jalapeño pepper, seeded and finely chopped
2 teaspoons ground cumin
4 onion rolls, split and toasted
Shredded lettuce for garnish
½ cup Tomato Salsa (page 93) or your favorite purchased brand

Prepare the grill.

In a medium bowl, use a fork to mash the bread, tomato paste, and water to a paste. Add the turkey, beans, coriander, thyme, and salt and pepper, and set aside.

In a small nonstick skillet, heat the oil over moderate heat. Add the onion and cook 6 minutes or until golden. Add the garlic, jalapeño, and cumin and cook for 2 minutes more. (If the mixture becomes too dry, add 1 tablespoon water.) Let the mixture cool, then add it to the turkey mixture and mix thoroughly but lightly. Shape into four ¾-inch patties. Grill the patties on a lightly oiled rack, set 4 inches over glowing coals, for 5 minutes a side or until they are completely cooked through. (Alternatively, broil the patties in a broiler 4 inches from the flame.)

Serve the burgers on the rolls garnished with the lettuce and the tomato salsa.

Nutritional Analysis *per serving: 298 calories; 31% calories from fat; 11 grams of fat; 468 milligrams of sodium*

SUPER-EASY CHICKEN OR BEEF FAJITAS

Fajitas are like a Pavlovian dinner bell to me. I see a fajita on a menu, and I start to drool. This recipe is so easy. Even better, my kids will eat it.

Makes 8 fajitas

2 tablespoons fresh lime juice
1 garlic clove, minced (about 1 teaspoon)
¼ teaspoon red pepper flakes
2 large whole boneless, skinless chicken breasts cut in half (about 1½ pounds total)
Salt and pepper to taste
3 bell peppers (red, green, or yellow or a mixture), cut into strips
1 onion, sliced
Nonstick vegetable oil spray
8 eight-inch flour tortillas
3 cups Quick Chili Beans (recipe page 196), heated
1 cup Tomato Salsa (page 93), or your favorite purchased brand
½ cup plain nonfat yogurt, or low-fat or nonfat sour cream
1 cup Guacamole (page 92), optional

Prepare the grill and preheat the oven to 450°F.

Mix together the first three ingredients. Brush the chicken with the mixture, sprinkle it with salt and pepper to taste, and grill it on a lightly oiled rack 4 inches above glowing coals about 5 minutes on each side, or until cooked through.

(Alternatively, broil the chicken on a rack in a preheated broiler about 4 inches from the heat.) Arrange the vegetables in one layer on a shallow roasting pan that has been sprayed lightly with nonstick vegetable oil spray. Roast them in the oven for 10 to 12 minutes, or until they are tender. Sprinkle them with salt and pepper to taste.

Wrap the tortillas in aluminum foil, and heat in the oven for 5 minutes. Slice the chicken thin and divide it among four plates. Arrange one-quarter of the pepper mixture, chili beans, salsa, yogurt, and guacamole next to the chicken. Serve with the heated tortillas.

To make beef fajitas: Substitute a 1½-pound piece of flank steak for the chicken, and grill it for 9 to 10 minutes per side. Let the meat rest for 10 minutes before slicing it very thin across the grain.

Nutritional Analysis *per chicken fajita: 305 calories; 17% calories from fat; 6 grams of fat; 451 milligrams of sodium*

Nutritional Analysis *per beef fajita: 336 calories; 27% calories from fat; 11 grams of fat; 459 milligrams of sodium*

JEWEL OF THE NILE
CHICKEN KEBABS

When Michael Douglas, Kathleen Turner, and Danny DeVito were in Fez, Morocco, shooting *Jewel of the Nile,* I was asked by *GMA* to go there to cover the filming of the movie. Michael Douglas and I in exotic North Africa . . . could it be? Well, at least I came home with this delicious recipe from the hotel, and it has been perfected by Patsy Jamieson.

Serves 6

FOR THE MARINADE:

½ cup plain nonfat yogurt
½ cup chopped fresh parsley
1 tablespoon chopped fresh coriander
¼ cup fresh lemon juice
2 tablespoons olive oil
1½ cloves garlic, minced (about 1½ teaspoons)
1 tablespoon paprika
1 tablespoon curry powder
2 teaspoons ground cumin
½ teaspoon salt
½ teaspoon freshly ground black pepper

FOR THE KEBABS:

1½ pounds boneless, skinless chicken breasts, cut into 1-inch pieces
1 small yellow or orange bell pepper cut into 1-inch pieces
1 yellow squash, cut into ¼-inch-thick rounds
2 small onions, cut into ½-inch wedges
12 cherry tomatoes
1 recipe Herbed Couscous with Lemon (page 142)

Prepare the grill.

In a bowl, stir together all the marinade ingredients, add the chicken, and toss to coat well. Chill, covered with plastic wrap, for 20 minutes. Drop the pepper into a pot of boiling water and blanch for 2 minutes, remove with a slotted spoon, and drain. Blanch the summer squash for 1 minute, remove with a slotted spoon, and drain.

Alternate chicken cubes, peppers, yellow squash, onions, and cherry tomatoes on 6 long skewers. Arrange the skewers on the prepared grill 4 to 6 inches from the glowing coals, and grill for 3 to 4 minutes per side or until the chicken is just cooked through. (The kebabs can also be broiled.) Serve with the couscous.

Nutritional Analysis *per kebab, including couscous: 352 calories; 20% calories from fat; 8 grams of fat; 312 milligrams of sodium*

Michael Douglas, Joan, Danny DeVito, Kathleen Turner

CHICKEN CACCIATORE OVER NOODLES

This is comfort food at its finest for all of us. And a little Chianti served with it adds an additionally pleasant "There, there." Yes, it's a dish I serve on special occasions.

Serves 4 to 6

1½ *pounds skinless, boneless chicken*
    breast halves, cut into ½-inch pieces
2 *tablespoons all-purpose flour seasoned*
    with salt and pepper for dusting
2 *tablespoons olive oil*
1 *medium onion, chopped (about 1 cup)*
3 *garlic cloves, minced (about 1 table-*
    spoon)
½ *pound mushrooms, wiped clean with a*
    damp cloth and halved or quartered if
    large
1 *green pepper, cut into ½-inch pieces*
1 *teaspoon dried thyme or rosemary*
½ *cup dry white wine*
16-*ounce can plum tomatoes, chopped,*
    juice reserved
1 *tablespoon tomato paste*
1½ *cups Chicken Broth (page 203) or*
    canned reduced-sodium chicken broth
¼ *cup chopped fresh parsley*
½ *pound boiled yolk-free egg noodles*
Salt and pepper to taste

Coat the chicken pieces with the flour and shake them in a strainer to get rid of the excess. Heat the oil in a large nonstick skillet over moderately high heat until hot. Add half the chicken, sauté it for 3 to 4 minutes or until it is lightly browned on all sides, and transfer it to a bowl with a slotted spoon. Repeat the procedure with the remaining chicken.

Add the onion and the garlic to the skillet and cook over moderately low heat for 5 minutes or until the onion is softened. Add the mushrooms, green pepper, and thyme or rosemary and cook for 5 minutes. Stir in the wine, tomatoes and their juice, tomato paste, and chicken broth and simmer the mixture for 30 minutes or until the liquid is reduced by half. Return the chicken to the pan and simmer for 3 minutes or until the chicken is just cooked through. Stir in the parsley and salt and pepper to taste, and serve each portion over a mound of yolk-free egg noodles.

Nutritional Analysis *per serving: 445 calories; 19% calories from fat; 9 grams of fat; 382 milligrams of sodium*

CHICKEN YUCATÁN

This recipe originated with chef Michael Willoughby. I found it through my friends at *Eating Well* magazine. Serve with potatoes, rice and beans, or plain rice. A large platter of fresh seasonal fruit, such as mangoes, grapes, melons, or papaya, complements the cumin-scented, citrusy sauce.

Serves 6

3 tablespoons fresh orange juice
2 tablespoons canned unsweetened pineap-
ple juice
2 tablespoons fresh lime juice
2 tablespoons chopped fresh oregano (or 2
teaspoons dried)
1 tablespoon olive oil
1 teaspoon ground cumin
1 teaspoon chili powder
1 garlic clove, chopped (about 1 teaspoon)
4 to 6 dashes hot sauce
Salt and pepper to taste
6 bone-in chicken thighs (2½ pounds
total), skin and fat removed

Preheat oven to 375°F.

In a food processor or blender, combine all the ingredients except the chicken, add salt and pepper to taste, and puree until smooth. Arrange the chicken in an 8×11½-inch baking dish, and brush with half the citrus-herb mixture. Bake the chicken in the preheated oven, turning once and brushing occasionally with the remaining mixture, for 30 to 35 minutes or until the chicken is no longer pink in the center. Season with salt and pepper to taste. Serve hot with Mom's Roasted New Potatoes (page 192; make 1½ recipes), or cold.

Nutritional Analysis *per serving: 385 calories; 35% calories from fat; 15 grams of fat; 86 milligrams of sodium*

MOM'S CREAMED CHICKEN OVER NOODLES

I grew up on this recipe. It's one of those cravings I took with me when I left Sacramento. I've lowered the fat and calories, which allows me to enjoy the flavor of this favorite almost guilt-free.

Serves 4

1 medium onion, chopped (about 1 cup),
   or 3 scallions, chopped fine
1 tablespoon unsalted butter
½ pound mushrooms, wiped clean with a
   damp cloth and sliced
1 tablespoon all-purpose flour
¾ cup Chicken Broth (page 203) or
   canned reduced-sodium chicken broth,
   heated
½ cup evaporated skim milk
2 teaspoons fresh lemon juice
1 tablespoon chopped fresh dill (or 1 teaspoon dried), optional
¼ cup low-fat sour cream
3 skinless, boneless chicken breast halves,
   poached (see procedure on page 117)
   and cut into bite-size pieces
Salt and pepper to taste
½ pound boiled egg noodles (or yolk-free
   egg noodles)

In a large nonstick skillet, cook the onion in the butter over moderately low heat for 5 minutes or until the onion is softened. Add the mushrooms, and cook the mixture over moderate heat for 8 to 10 minutes, or until almost all of the liquid the mushrooms give off is evaporated. Sprinkle the flour over the mushrooms and cook the mixture, stirring, for 2 minutes. Whisk in the broth, bring the mixture to a boil, whisking, and simmer it for 3 minutes. Add the milk, and simmer the mixture for 3 to 5 minutes or until it is thickened. Stir in the lemon juice, the dill (if using), the sour cream, the chicken, and salt and pepper to taste, and cook the mixture over moderate heat until it is heated through. Serve each portion over a mound of the noodles.

Variations:
   • Add 2 tablespoons of white wine with the chicken broth.
   • Add half of a green or red pepper, chopped, with the mushrooms.
   • Stir in 1 tablespoon of curry powder with the onion to make a chicken curry, and garnish the dish with sliced banana, sliced papaya, a few crushed peanuts, and a little shredded coconut.

Nutritional Analysis *per serving: 456 calories; 18% calories from fat; 9 grams of fat; 261 milligrams of sodium*

SAMI'S MUSTARD CHICKEN

This recipe came to me from my former personal assistant Samantha "Sami" Berg. Sami was never one who spent a lot of time in the kitchen, so you know this must be quick and easy to make. The chopped green chilies pack a little punch, so if you don't like spicy foods, make those optional.

Serves 6

1 cup Low-Fat Ranch Dressing (page 124) or your favorite purchased low-fat or nonfat dressing
2 tablespoons Dijon mustard
4-ounce can chopped green chilies, drained
1 tablespoon olive oil
1 red bell pepper, cut into thin strips
1 medium onion, chopped (about 1 cup)
1½ pounds boneless, skinless chicken breasts cut into strips (about 1½ inches × ¼ inch)
3 cups cooked rice
1 tablespoon chopped parsley

In a bowl, whisk together the dressing, mustard, and chilies.

In a large nonstick skillet, heat the oil over moderately high heat until it is hot. Add the onion and the red pepper, and stir-fry for 3 minutes. Add the chicken, and stir-fry for 5 more minutes or until the chicken is just cooked through. Add the dressing mixture, and cook until it is hot. Serve the chicken over the rice sprinkled with the parsley.

Nutritional Analysis *per serving: 366 calories; 24% calories from fat; 10 grams of fat; 560 milligrams of sodium*

TURKEY MEATLOAF

I grew up on meatloaf. But in these calorie-conscious times, Ruth Spear's simple-to-prepare version is a lower-fat alternative. I think it's light, moist, and divine. Pretty exotic description for meatloaf, don't you think? Try it and decide for yourself.

Serves 4 to 6

FOR THE MEATLOAF:
⅓ cup bread crumbs
⅓ cup skim milk
1¼ pounds ground raw turkey
1 egg white, beaten lightly
*1 small onion, finely chopped or grated
    (about ½ cup)*
*1 garlic clove, minced (about 1 teaspoon),
    optional*
½ small green bell pepper, chopped fine
3 tablespoons catsup
½ teaspoon dried oregano
½ teaspoon ground cumin
Salt and pepper to taste

FOR THE GLAZE:
3 tablespoons brown sugar
¼ cup catsup
1 teaspoon dry mustard

Preheat the oven to 350°F.

In a large bowl, combine the bread crumbs and the milk, add the turkey, and mix well. Stir in the egg white, onion, garlic (if using), green pepper, catsup, oregano, cumin, and salt and pepper to taste. Transfer the mixture to a 9×5×3-inch loaf pan, rap it once on the counter to settle the meat, and smooth the top lightly with the back of a fork.

Bake the meatloaf in the preheated oven for 40 minutes. The loaf will have shrunk a bit and a savory liquid collected in the dish; carefully spoon this out to use later over the meatloaf as gravy.

In a bowl, stir together the sugar, catsup, and mustard, and spread over the top of the meatloaf. Bake 20 minutes more, and then let the meatloaf stand for 5 minutes before slicing. Serve with the reserved savory liquid.

Nutritional Analysis *per serving: 188 calories; 36% calories
from fat; 8 grams of fat; 256 milligrams of sodium*

BARBECUED TURKEY BREAST

A twist on the traditional turkey breast, this one will knock your socks off. It came from Laura's cousin Karen Weiss, a mother with four kids who's also a busy CPA. If she can whip this up, so can you.

Serves 16

FOR THE MARINADE:
4 garlic cloves, minced (about 4 tea-
spoons)
2 tablespoons minced fresh ginger root
1½ tablespoons poppy seeds
2 scallions, minced
1½ cups reduced-sodium soy sauce
¼ cup olive oil
2 tablespoons rice wine vinegar
Juice of 3 lemons
½ teaspoon freshly ground pepper

4-pound boneless turkey breast with the
skin on

FOR THE GLAZE:
½ cup apricot preserves
½ cup Dijon mustard
1 teaspoon minced fresh ginger root

In a large bowl, whisk together all the marinade ingredients. Add the turkey, turn to coat it well with the marinade, and let it marinate, covered and chilled, overnight.

Prepare the grill.

In a saucepan, heat the ingredients for the glaze over moderately low heat until the apricot preserves are melted. Keep it warm.

Remove the turkey from the marinade and pat it dry. Arrange it, skin side down, on a rack set 6 inches from the glowing coals, and grill it for 15 to 20 minutes. Turn it over, and grill it for an additional 10 to 15 minutes. Grill each side for another 5 minutes after brushing it with the warm glaze. (Check to make sure the turkey is just cooked through; if it isn't, grill it an additional 5 minutes.) Let the turkey breast stand for 10 minutes before carving.

Nutritional Analysis per serving: 153 calories; 26% calories
from fat; 4 grams of fat; 626 milligrams of sodium

Chapter 11

F I S H

WOLFGANG PUCK'S ROASTED SALMON WITH HERB CRUST

Los Angeles restauranteur and chef extraordinaire Wolfgang Puck is always a popular guest on *GMA,* because we know we are in for a treat with his cooking. After he demonstrated how to make this dish on the show, everyone in the studio asked for a copy of the recipe. Once you try it, you'll see why. We adapted this from Wolfgang's original recipe, and it's one of my favorites.

Serves 6

FOR THE TOMATO FONDUE:
1 medium onion, chopped (about 1 cup)
6 garlic cloves, minced (about 2 table-
spoons)
1 tablespoon extra-virgin olive oil
3 pounds ripe tomatoes, peeled,* seeded,
and chopped
¼ cup dry white wine
1 tablespoon tomato paste
2 tablespoons each of finely chopped fresh
thyme and parsley
3 tablespoons chopped fresh basil leaves
Salt and pepper to taste

FOR THE POTATO PUREE:
3 large baking potatoes (about 2 to 2¼
pounds total), peeled and quartered
½ cup fresh basil leaves, blanched in boil-
ing water for 5 seconds and cooled in
ice water
1 tablespoon extra-virgin olive oil
⅔ cup 1% milk

FOR THE ROASTED SALMON:
¾ cup dry bread crumbs
4 tablespoons coarsely grated fresh horse-
radish
3 tablespoons freshly chopped fresh herb
mixture (a combination of any of the
following: dill, parsley, tarragon,
thyme, chives, or basil)
1 tablespoon extra-virgin olive oil
6 six-ounce pieces salmon fillets, skinned
6 basil sprigs for garnish

Preheat the oven to 500°F.

Make the fondue: In a skillet, cook the onion and the garlic in the olive oil over moderately low heat, covered, for 5 minutes, or until softened. Add the tomatoes, the wine, and the tomato paste, bring to a boil, and simmer about 20 minutes or until the sauce thickens.

Stir in the herbs and salt and pepper to taste. Transfer the mixture to a food processor or blender, and puree until smooth. (The tomato sauce may be made several days in advance, kept covered and chilled, and then reheated.)

Make the potato puree: In a saucepan, combine the potatoes with lightly salted water to cover, bring to a boil, and simmer until tender. In a blender, puree the basil with the oil and 3 tablespoons of the milk. Drain the potatoes and pass them through a food mill fitted with the fine blade. Stir in the milk, basil puree, and salt and pepper to taste. Keep the potatoes warm in a double boiler.

Make the roasted salmon: In a bowl, toss together the crumbs, horseradish, and herb mixture. Season the salmon with salt and pepper to taste, and pat one-sixth of the herb mixture on top of each piece. Drizzle the oil over the crumbs. Arrange the fillets in a shallow baking pan, and roast them in the oven for 8 to 10 minutes, or until just cooked through. Divide the potato puree evenly in the center of six plates, and place the salmon on top. Spoon the tomato fondue around the fish, and garnish each plate with a basil sprig.

*To peel a fresh tomato, plunge it into boiling water for 30 seconds, and immediately transfer it with a slotted spoon to a bowl of ice and water. If the peel does not come off easily, return the tomato to the boiling water for another 10 to 20 seconds.

Nutritional Analysis *per serving: 492 calories; 26% calories from fat; 14 grams of fat; 371 milligrams of sodium*

Joan and Wolfgang Puck

EASY SALMON AND VEGETABLES IN FOIL

I love this dish because you can make it ahead of time, saving any last-minute fuss. Just before dinner, pop the foil envelopes into the oven. Dinner's ready in 15 to 20 minutes.

Serves 4

4 six-ounce pieces salmon fillets (about ½-inch thick)
4 teaspoons fresh lemon juice
2 teaspoons finely chopped fresh ginger, optional
Salt and pepper to taste
2 tablespoons extra-virgin olive oil
2 red potatoes, boiled until just tender and sliced
1 cup snow peas, blanched in boiling water for 30 seconds and drained
2 carrots, thinly sliced and blanched in boiling water for 1 minute
¼ small zucchini, sliced
¼ small fennel bulb, thinly sliced, optional
4 teaspoons chopped fresh dill, basil, thyme, or parsley for garnish

Preheat the oven to 400°F.

Cut four sheets of aluminum foil into rectangles, approximately 10×16 inches. Arrange one piece of salmon in the middle of each sheet, slightly to the left of center. Sprinkle one teaspoon of lemon juice and ½ teaspoon ginger (if using) over each piece of salmon, and season with salt and pepper to taste. Top each salmon fillet with one-fourth of the olive oil, and one-fourth of each of the vegetables. Fold the foil over the salmon to form a rectangle, and crimp all the edges tightly. (The recipe may be prepared to this point a couple of hours ahead and refrigerated, but the cooking time should be increased by 5 minutes.)

Bake the foil packets on cookie sheets in the preheated oven for 15 minutes or until the salmon is just cooked through. To serve, place a packet on each of four dinner plates, slash an X in each to open it up, and sprinkle with some of the fresh chopped herbs.

Note: Optional alternative vegetables include 1 cup peas, 1 cup corn, 8 stalks blanched small asparagus, ¼ cup sliced rehydrated* sundried tomatoes (not oil-packed).

*To rehydrate tomatoes: Pour boiling water over the tomatoes (to cover) and let them stand for 20 minutes. Drain and pat dry.

Nutritional Analysis *per serving: 358 calories; 32% calories from fat; 13 grams of fat; 126 milligrams of sodium*

BAKED FILLET OF SOLE
WITH SALSA

The snappy flavor of salsa has always been one of my favorites. Maybe it's because I have spent a great deal of time in Mexico. Maybe I just like hot, spicy food. Who knows . . . who cares? Just try it on baked sole and see if you don't love it, too. Pick up some fresh fish on your way home from work, and you have the making of a very quick, very lean entree.

Serves 4

1 cup Tomato Salsa (page 93) or your favorite purchased brand
4 six-ounce pieces sole fillets
Salt and pepper to taste

Preheat the oven to 350°F.

In a shallow baking dish, just large enough to hold the sole in one layer, spread one-half of the salsa. Arrange the fish in one layer on top of the salsa, season with salt and pepper, and bake for 7 minutes. Spread the remaining salsa on top of the fish, and bake for an additional 7 to 8 minutes or until it is just cooked through.

Nutritional Analysis *per serving: 154 calories; 12% calories from fat; 2 grams of fat; 129 milligrams of sodium*

BROILED FILLET OF SOLE WITH LEMON AND CAPERS

Dinner doesn't get much quicker than this — unless your specialty is making reservations. Watch the clock while the fish is broiling, or it'll cook to a crisp.

Serves 4

4 six-ounce sole fillets
2 teaspoons lemon pepper
2 teaspoons dried dill
1 teaspoon garlic powder, or to taste
4 teaspoons capers
1 tablespoon fresh lemon juice
Salt and pepper to taste
12 thin lemon slices

Preheat the broiler.

Arrange the fish in one layer on a baking sheet, and sprinkle each fillet with one-fourth of the lemon pepper, dill, garlic powder, capers, and lemon juice. Season with salt and pepper to taste, and arrange 3 lemon slices on top of each one. Broil on a rack set 4 inches from the heat for 6 minutes, or until they are just cooked through.

Nutritional Analysis *per serving: 153 calories; 12% calories from fat; 2 grams of fat; 605 milligrams of sodium*

B. SMITH'S GRILLED SEAFOOD BROCHETTES

B. Smith

A former cover girl for *Harper's Bazaar* and *Vogue,* this high-fashion model can cook, too. No wonder her namesake restaurants in New York and Washington, D.C., are a hit. She won everyone over at our studio with her vivaciousness and her tasty cooking. This lower-fat version of her original recipe tastes great and is fun to make, too!

Serves 4

FOR THE MARINADE:

¼ cup olive oil
2 tablespoons fresh lemon juice
1 garlic clove, minced (about 1 teaspoon)
1 teaspoon ground ginger
¼ teaspoon salt
¼ teaspoon ground black pepper

FOR THE BROCHETTES:

8 large shrimp (about ½ pound), peeled and deveined
8 sea scallops (about ½ pound)
½ pound fresh tuna, cut into 8 pieces
½ large green bell pepper cut into ½-inch pieces
2 small onions, cut into ½-inch-thick wedges
8 cherry tomatoes
Lemon wedges for garnish

Prepare the grill.

In a large bowl, whisk together all the marinade ingredients. Rinse the seafood, and pat it dry with paper towels. Add it to the marinade, and toss the mixture until all the seafood is coated well. Chill, covered, for 1 to 2 hours, stirring occasionally.

Thread the seafood, bell pepper, onions, and tomatoes onto four long skewers. Grill the brochettes on a prepared grill, 4 to 6 inches from the glowing coals, for about 3 minutes on each side, or until the seafood is just cooked through. (Alternatively, broil the fish on a rack 4 inches from the preheated broiler.) Serve immediately, garnished with lemon wedges.

Nutritional Analysis *per serving: 229 calories; 23% calories from fat; 6 grams of fat; 290 milligrams of sodium*

GRILLED SWORDFISH

(OR SALMON)

Since swordfish is one of my favorite fish, I had to include a recipe — and this one's a classic case of "less is more." Don't substitute ground ginger for fresh ginger root; they impart different flavors.

Serves 6

4 tablespoons reduced-sodium soy sauce
2 garlic cloves, minced (about 2 teaspoons)
2 teaspoons sugar
4 teaspoons fresh lemon juice
2 teaspoons grated fresh ginger root,
    optional
¼ to ½ teaspoon red pepper flakes, or to
    taste
6 six-ounce pieces swordfish steak (or
    salmon fillet)
Nonstick vegetable oil spray

Prepare the grill.

In a bowl, whisk together the soy sauce, garlic, sugar, lemon juice, ginger root (if using), and red pepper flakes. Arrange the fish in one layer in a shallow dish, pour the marinade over it, and chill, covered, for 30 minutes.

Remove the fish from the marinade, and pat it dry. Grill the fish on a rack sprayed with the nonstick vegetable oil spray, set 4 inches from the glowing coals, for 3 to 4 minutes a side or until it is just cooked though.

Nutritional Analysis *per serving: 208 calories; 31% calories from fat; 7 grams of fat; 193 milligrams of sodium*

SAUTÉED RED SNAPPER WITH MANGO SALSA

If *GMA*'s entertainment editor, Joel Siegel, were reviewing the recipes here, he'd refer to this one as a "sleeper." It doesn't sound nearly as good as it is. The combination of flavors in this winning dish comes to life in your mouth.

Serves 4

FOR THE SALSA:

1 firm-ripe medium mango, peeled, pitted, and finely chopped (about 2 cups)
½ small red onion, chopped fine, soaked in cold water for 20 minutes, and drained
1 jalapeño, minced, or 1 teaspoon hot sauce
3 tablespoons fresh lime juice
2 tablespoons chopped fresh coriander or basil
Salt and pepper to taste

FOR THE FISH:

4 teaspoons vegetable oil
4 six-ounce red snapper fillets, skinned
Juice of half a lemon

In a bowl, combine all the salsa ingredients well, and chill the mixture for at least 30 minutes or up to 1 hour.

In a large nonstick skillet, heat the oil over moderately high heat until it is hot. Add the fish, and sauté it for 3 to 4 minutes a side or until it is just cooked through. Sprinkle with the lemon juice, and salt and pepper to taste, and top each portion with some of the salsa.

Nutritional Analysis *per serving: 258 calories; 25% calories from fat; 7 grams of fat; 77 milligrams of sodium*

PAN-SEARED ORANGE CHILI
SCALLOPS

I like scallops when they're browned. That's why I chose to include a pan-seared recipe in my book. The marinade is especially good, mixing the sweet and sour flavors of traditional Mandarin cooking.

Serves 4

FOR THE MARINADE:
1 garlic clove, minced (about 1 teaspoon)
1½ tablespoons rice wine vinegar
1 tablespoon reduced-sodium soy sauce
Freshly grated orange rind from 2 small
  oranges (about 1½ to 2 teaspoons)

1 pound sea scallops, rinsed and patted
  dry

FOR THE SAUCE:
2 teaspoons Chinese chili paste
Juice of 2 small oranges (about ⅔ cup)
2 teaspoons brown sugar
1 tablespoon reduced-sodium soy sauce
Pinch of red pepper flakes
1 teaspoon cornstarch

1 tablespoon vegetable oil
½ pound snow peas, blanched in boiling
  water for 30 seconds and drained
2 carrots, thinly sliced, blanched in boil-
  ing water for 2 minutes and drained
2 cups cooked white rice as an accompa-
  niment, if desired

In a bowl, whisk together all the marinade ingredients, add the scallops, and marinate, covered, for 20 minutes. In a bowl, whisk together all the ingredients for the sauce.

Remove the scallops from the marinade, reserving the marinade, and pat the scallops dry. In a large nonstick skillet, heat the oil over high heat until it is just smoking. Add the scallops, and sauté for 2 to 3 minutes or until they are lightly browned on both sides and cooked through. Season with salt and freshly ground pepper, if desired, and transfer with a slotted spoon to a plate.

Add the sauce and the reserved marinade to the skillet. Bring to a boil and simmer for 2 minutes. Add the snow peas and carrots, and cook for 1 minute. Divide the scallops among four plates, and spoon the sauce and vegetables over them. Serve with the rice.

Nutritional Analysis *per serving: 338 calories; 13% calories from fat; 5 grams of fat; 410 milligrams of sodium*

WOLFGANG PUCK'S TUNA WITH GRILLED SUMMER VEGETABLE SALSA

L.A.'s best-known restaurateur pulls off another winning combination with this fresh tuna for summer dining. It's as pretty as it is delicious.

Serves 8

8 six-ounce pieces tuna steaks (cut about
   1 inch thick)
1 red bell pepper, halved
1 yellow bell pepper, halved
1 small fennel bulb, cut into ⅓-inch-thick
   slices
1 very small eggplant, cut into ½-inch-
   thick slices
1 ear of corn, shucked
1 small onion, cut into ⅓-inch-thick slices
1 small zucchini or yellow squash, cut
   lengthwise into ½-inch-thick slices
Nonstick vegetable oil spray
1 jalapeño, roasted,* peeled, and seeded
⅔ cup fresh lime juice
⅓ cup packed coriander leaves, rinsed
   and spun dry
2 teaspoons ground cumin
1½ cups cherry tomatoes, halved
¼ cup extra-virgin olive oil
Salt and pepper to taste

Prepare the grill.

Lightly spray all the vegetables except the tomatoes with the nonstick vegetable oil spray and arrange them in one layer, in batches if necessary, on an oiled rack set 5 to 6 inches over glowing coals. Grill the vegetables, turning occasionally, for 10 to 20 minutes or until they are just tender. The cooking time will vary according to the vegetable. (Alternatively, grill the vegetables on an oiled ridged grill pan, or broil them in a preheated broiler 5 to 6 inches from the heat.) As the vegetables are done, transfer them to a platter to cool; when they are cool enough to be handled, coarsely chop them.

In a blender, combine the jalapeño, lime juice, half the coriander, and half the cumin, and blend until smooth. In a bowl, combine the chopped vegetables, tomatoes, cumin, remaining coriander, and olive oil. Stir in the blended jalapeño mixture, and toss the mixture well. Season with salt and pepper to taste.

Grill the tuna on an oiled rack set 5 to 6 inches over glowing coals (about 3 minutes on each side for medium-rare fish). Season with salt and pepper to taste and top each steak with one-eighth of the mixture.

To roast the jalapeño: Using a long-handled fork, char the pepper over an open flame or on a rack set over an electric burner, turning until the skin is blackened, about 4 to 6 minutes. (Alternatively, broil the pepper on the rack of a broiler pan under a preheated broiler about 2 inches from heat, turning every 5 minutes until the skin is blistered and charred.) Transfer the pepper to a bowl and let it stand, covered, until cool enough to handle. When cool, remove the skin.

Nutritional Analysis *per serving: 452 calories; 46% calories from fat; 23 grams of fat; 83 milligrams of sodium*

CRAB CAKES

In the fall of 1994, *GMA* set sail across the Chesapeake Bay to launch one of its famous bus trips through the Northeast. As the sun rose over the bay, the lighthouse in the distance and the taste of these crab cakes created a picture-perfect beginning.

Serves 4 as a main course or 12 as an appetizer

¼ cup low-fat mayonnaise
¼ cup finely chopped celery (or red or green bell pepper)
¼ cup finely chopped scallion
¼ cup finely chopped parsley
2 tablespoons fresh lemon juice
1 teaspoon hot sauce, or to taste
1 teaspoon Dijon mustard, or to taste
1-pound lump crabmeat, picked over, or imitation crabmeat, flaked
1 cup dry bread crumbs
Salt and pepper to taste
2 teaspoons vegetable oil
½ cup Tomato Salsa (page 93) or Spicy Tomato Sauce (page 181) as an accompaniment

In a large bowl, combine the first eight ingredients, ¼ cup of the bread crumbs, and salt and pepper to taste. Form the mixture into eight patties (the mixture will be soft), and coat each patty with some of the remaining bread crumbs.

In a large nonstick skillet, cook the crab cakes in the oil over moderate heat for about 3 minutes a side or until they are golden. Transfer them to plates, and top each portion with some of the salsa.

Note: To make appetizer-size crab cakes, divide the mixture into twelve little mounds, shape each mound into a small patty, and cook in the same manner, but only for 2 to 3 minutes a side.

Nutritional Analysis *per main-course serving: 299 calories; 32% calories from fat; 11 grams of fat; 989 milligrams of sodium*

Nutritional Analysis *per 1 appetizer-size crab cake: 100 calories; 32% calories from fat; 4 grams of fat; 330 milligrams of sodium*

Chapter 12

❖

MEATLESS MAIN DISHES
VEGETARIAN SHEPHERD'S PIE

In 1990, I took all three of my girls on a *GMA* trip through England, Scotland, and Ireland. Finding food that the girls would eat was definitely my most difficult assignment. I felt like Columbus discovering America when I stumbled upon Shepherd's Pie. Mashed potatoes and ground round — how could I go wrong? But when your teenage daughter decides she's a vegetarian, what's a mother to do? I turned to Steven Raichlen, author of the award-winning *Low-Fat, High-Flavor Vegetarian Cooking,* for this recipe.

Serves 4 to 6

FOR THE MASHED POTATOES:

2 baking potatoes (1¼ to 1½ pounds total), peeled and cut into quarters

¼ cup low-fat or nonfat sour cream

Salt and pepper to taste

1 cup to 1¼ cups Vegetable Stock (page 204) or Chicken Broth (page 203), or canned reduced-sodium chicken broth

FOR THE REST OF THE PIE:

1 medium onion, finely chopped (about 1 cup)

1 tablespoon olive oil

2 garlic cloves, minced (about 2 teaspoons)

1 teaspoon ground cumin

4 carrots, thinly sliced

1½ cups stewed tomatoes, chopped, reserving the juice

2 tablespooons tomato paste

1½ cups cooked corn kernels

1½ cups cooked peas

15-ounce can kidney beans, drained and rinsed

Preheat the oven to 400°F.

Make the mashed potatoes: In a saucepan, combine the potatoes with water to cover by 2 inches. Bring the water to a boil and cook the potatoes for 20 minutes or until they are tender. Drain the potatoes well, and put them through a food mill fitted with the fine blade, or a potato ricer. Stir in the sour cream, salt and pepper to taste, and ¼ to ½ cup of the stock, or enough to make a smooth, moist puree.

In a large nonstick skillet, cook the onion in the oil over moderately low heat for 5 minutes or until it is softened. Add the garlic, the cumin, and the carrots and cook the mixture, covered, for 5 minutes. Add the tomatoes with their juice, the tomato paste, and the remaining ¾ cup of the stock, and simmer the mixture until it is reduced by half. Stir in the corn, peas, kidney beans, and salt and pepper to taste.

Pour the vegetable mixture into a deep 10-inch quiche pan, and smooth the potato mixture on the top. Bake the pie in the preheated oven for 20 minutes or until the filling is bubbling.

(The pie may be made a day ahead and kept chilled. If made ahead, bake for an additional 10 minutes to reheat.)

Nutritional Analysis *per serving: 402 calories; 13% calories from fat; 6 grams of fat; 546 milligrams of sodium*

MEAN BEAN CHILI

This was inspired by Laura's Aunt Eunice from Detroit, Michigan. I never found a vegetarian chili I liked better. Thanks, Eunie! The absence of meat whittles away at the fat; the canned beans certainly add to the convenience, but do up the sodium count. Try buying reduced-sodium tomato sauce and beans to cut the sodium level. For those on a restricted-sodium diet, simply start with beans cooked from scratch.

Makes about 11 to 12 cups

2 large onions, chopped (about 3 cups)
6 garlic cloves, minced (about 2 table-
    spoons)
2 tablespoons olive oil
1 tablespoon chili powder
2 teaspoons dried oregano
2 teaspoons dried basil
1 teaspoon ground cumin
½ teaspoon cayenne
5 fifteen-ounce cans beans (kidney, pinto,
    etc.), rinsed and drained
28-ounce can low-sodium tomatoes,
    chopped, juice reserved
26-ounce jar of your favorite purchased
    spaghetti sauce (such as Healthy
    Choice)
6 dashes hot sauce, or to taste
1 to 2 cups water

OPTIONAL ADDITIONS:
1½ pounds lean ground raw turkey*
1 tablespoon Liquid Smoke

In a large kettle, preferably nonstick, cook the onion and the garlic in the oil over moderately low heat for 5 minutes, or until the onion is softened. Add the chili powder, oregano, basil, cumin, and cayenne, and cook for 3 minutes. Add the beans, tomatoes, spaghetti sauce, hot sauce, and enough water to cover the beans. Bring the mixture to a boil and simmer it, stirring occasionally, for 45 minutes.

If using the turkey, cook in a nonstick pan over moderately low heat until it is no longer pink. Also, add an additional 26-ounce jar of spaghetti sauce.

Nutritional Analysis *per 1-cup serving: 181 calories; 16% calories from fat; 3 grams of fat; 211 milligrams of sodium*

SPINACH FRITTATA WITH SPICY TOMATO SAUCE

You don't have to be a vegetarian to love this excellent quiche alternative. Like an omelet, you can vary this according to your family's preferences.

Serves 4

FOR THE SAUCE:

2 medium tomatoes, coarsely chopped (about 2 cups)
½ medium onion, chopped (about ½ cup)
2 tablespoons chopped celery
2 tablespoons chopped green pepper
1 teaspoon paprika
4 to 6 dashes of hot sauce, or to taste
Salt and pepper to taste

FOR THE FRITTATA:

½ medium onion, chopped (about ½ cup)
2 teaspoons olive or vegetable oil
4 ounces spinach, coarse stems removed, rinsed and spun dry (about 3 cups)
1½ cups cholesterol-free egg product, or 4 large eggs and 4 large egg whites (lightly beaten)
1 tablespoon chopped fresh dill
2 tablespoons low-fat mozzarella or cheddar cheese, coarsely grated

Preheat the broiler.

Combine all the sauce ingredients in a saucepan, bring to a boil, and simmer for 15 to 20 minutes or until the sauce is thickened. Add salt and pepper to taste.

In a 10-inch nonstick skillet, cook the onion in the oil over moderately low heat for 5 minutes or until the onion is softened. Turn up the heat to moderate, add the spinach, and cook the mixture for 2 minutes or until the spinach is wilted. In a bowl, combine the egg product or the eggs with the dill, and salt and pepper to taste, and pour the mixture over the spinach. Cover and cook for 6 to 8 minutes or until the eggs are just set. Sprinkle the cheese over the top and broil for 1 minute or until it is golden on top. Serve each portion with some of the tomato sauce.

Nutritional Analysis *per serving: 145 calories; 37% calories from fat; 6 grams of fat; 209 milligrams of sodium*

EGGPLANT PARMESAN

I always thought that Eggplant Parmesan was fattening, but this version proved me wrong. Enjoy all the flavors of this classic dish, without all the fat. Serve with my Sautéed Portobellos with Warmed Field Greens for a very special dinner.

Serves 4

2 small eggplants (about 2 pounds total)
Nonstick vegetable oil spray
Juice of 1 lemon
Salt and pepper to taste
1½ cups Roasted Fresh Tomato Sauce
(page 197) or your favorite purchased
brand
4 ounces nonfat or low-fat mozzarella,
coarsely grated
¼ cup chopped parsley
⅓ cup freshly grated Parmesan (about 2½
ounces)

Preheat the oven to 400°F.

Peel the eggplants and slice them crosswise ¼-inch thick. Arrange the slices in one layer on a baking sheet sprayed with the nonstick vegetable oil spray, and sprinkle them with the lemon juice and salt and pepper to taste. Bake them for 10 minutes; turn them over and bake them for an additional 10 minutes or until golden.

Spread 2 tablespoons of the tomato sauce in the bottom of an 8-inch round quiche pan or pie plate. Arrange one-half of the eggplant slices over the sauce, overlapping them slightly, and top the eggplant with half of the remaining tomato sauce, half of the mozzarella, half of the parsley, and half of the Parmesan. Repeat the procedure with the remaining ingredients, and bake the Eggplant Parmesan in the preheated oven for 30 minutes or until very hot and bubbly.

(The Eggplant Parmesan can be made ahead and reheated at 350°F. for 30 to 40 minutes.)

Nutritional Analysis *per serving: 205 calories; 25% calories from fat; 6 grams of fat; 381 milligrams of sodium*

JAMIE'S VEGETABLE BURRITOS

Jamie Krauss

My daughter Jamie found this recipe at a Mexican restaurant near her summer camp in New Hampshire. It's been a challenge to learn how to cook to meet her vegetarian needs, but our entire family has benefited from it. Thanks, Jamie.

Makes 8 burritos

1 medium onion, cut into ⅓-inch-thick slices
1 green bell pepper, quartered
1 small summer squash (about 6 ounces), cut lengthwise into ⅓-inch-thick slices
1 small zucchini (about 6 ounces), cut lengthwise into ⅓-inch-thick slices
½ cup Reduced-Fat Italian Dressing (page 124) or your favorite purchased low-fat or nonfat brand
½ pound mushrooms, stems discarded and caps wiped clean with a damp cloth
8 ten-inch flour tortillas
½ recipe Quick Chili Beans (page 196), heated and mashed
1½ cups reduced-fat cheddar or Monterey Jack cheese, coarsely grated

Prepare the grill.

In a large shallow pan, toss all the vegetables except the mushrooms with the dressing. (Make sure the onion slices don't separate into rings.) Let the vegetables marinate for 10 minutes. Add the mushrooms, toss them to coat with the dressing, and marinate for an additional 10 minutes.

Remove the vegetables from the marinade and grill them on a rack set 4 inches above the glowing coals for at least 10 minutes a side, or until they are tender. (The peppers will take a little longer.) Alternatively, the vegetables can be broiled. Chop all the vegetables, and toss them together.

Preheat the oven to 400°F.

Arrange the tortillas in one layer on a couple of baking sheets, sprinkle 3 tablespoons of the cheese on top of each one, and bake the tortillas for 3 minutes or just until the cheese is melted. Spread ½ cup of the grilled vegetables and 3 tablespoons of the beans on each tortilla and roll up the burrito tightly, folding in the edges.

Nutritional Analysis *per 1-burrito serving: 193 calories; 25% calories from fat; 6 grams of fat; 406 milligrams of sodium*

Z U C C H I N I   B O A T S

Inspired by a trip to the Doral Saturnia Spa in Miami, where *GMA* was broadcast live for a week, this is one of those recipes that taught me how to eat skinny and stay skinny.

Serves 4

FOR THE FILLING:

1 cup cooked chopped spinach
½ medium onion, chopped fine (about ½ cup), blanched in boiling water for 1 minute and cooled
2 teaspoons dried oregano
3 cups cooked white or brown rice
2 cups low-fat cottage or ricotta cheese
Salt and pepper to taste

FOR THE REST:

4 medium zucchini, each about 8 inches long
Nonstick vegetable oil spray
1 cup Roasted Fresh Tomato Sauce (page 197) or your favorite purchased brand
3 ounces low-fat mozzarella, coarsely grated

Preheat the oven to 400°F.

In a bowl, toss together all the filling ingredients with salt and pepper to taste.

Cut off the ends of the zucchini and halve them lengthwise. Using a spoon, remove the seeds. Arrange the zucchini halves cut side down on a sheet pan that has been lightly sprayed with the nonstick vegetable oil spray, and roast them for 8 to 10 minutes or until they are just tender.

Mound one-eighth of the filling in the cavity of each zucchini boat. Return the boats to the oven and heat for 10 minutes. Top each with ⅛ cup of the tomato sauce and one-eighth of the mozzarella cheese, and bake for 5 more minutes.

Nutritional Analysis *per serving: 418 calories; 14% calories from fat; 6 grams of fat; 592 milligrams of sodium*

JEFF'S BLACK BEANS AND RICE

My brother, Jeff, has always liked to cook. While serving in the Navy, he lived in Puerto Rico for three years, and added this to his recipe collection. You can serve this dish as a main course, as an accompaniment to fajitas or burritos, or as a side dish to grilled meat or poultry.

Serves 6

2 cups *Chicken Broth (page 203) or canned reduced-sodium chicken broth*
1 cup *long grain rice*
1 medium *onion, chopped fine (about 1 cup)*
2 garlic *cloves, minced (about 2 teaspoons)*
2 teaspoons *olive oil*
2 sixteen-ounce *cans black beans, drained and rinsed*
1 cup *canned crushed tomatoes*
2 tablespoons *red wine vinegar*
¼ teaspoon *cayenne or to taste*
2 to 3 tablespoons *chopped fresh coriander, or to taste*
Salt and pepper to taste

In a saucepan, combine the chicken broth and the rice and bring to a boil. Reduce the heat to low, cover tightly, and simmer for 18 to 20 minutes, or until the rice is tender and the liquid has been absorbed.

While the rice is cooking, in a large nonstick skillet cook the onion and the garlic in the oil over moderate heat for 5 minutes, or until the onion is softened. Add the beans, tomatoes, vinegar, and cayenne, and simmer for 5 minutes. Stir in the reserved rice, coriander, and salt and pepper to taste.

Nutritional Analysis *per serving: 213 calories; 14% calories from fat; 4 grams of fat; 565 milligrams of sodium*

Chapter 13

❖

VEGETABLE SIDE DISHES

JULIA CHILD'S PUREE OF PARSNIPS

I really adore the flavor of parsnips and the texture of mashed potatoes. Leave it to Julia Child to combine two of my favorite things into one easy dish.

Serves 4 to 6

2 pounds parsnips, peeled and sliced
   about ⅓ inch thick
1 teaspoon salt
5 tablespoons heavy cream
2 tablespoons unsalted butter
Salt and freshly ground white pepper to
   taste

In a saucepan, combine the parsnips and salt with enough water to just cover them. Bring to a boil and simmer for 20 to 30 minutes, or until the parsnips are tender and most of the water has evaporated. Using a food mill fitted with the fine blade, or a food processor, puree the mixture and return it to the saucepan. Beat in the cream and butter, and season to taste with salt and freshly ground white pepper. Set the pan over another containing simmering water, cover and let cook for 20 to 30 minutes more. (The parsnip puree improves in flavor with this additional cooking.)

Nutritional Analysis *per serving: 199 calories; 38% calories from fat; 9 grams of fat; 376 milligrams of sodium*

❖

OUR VERSION OF JULIA CHILD'S PARSNIP PUREE

Serves 4 to 6

2 pounds parsnips, peeled and sliced
   about ⅓ inch thick
1 teaspoon salt
1 to 2 tablespoons unsalted butter cut into
   bits, optional
Salt and freshly ground white pepper to
   taste

In a saucepan, combine the parsnips and salt and enough water to just cover them. Bring to a boil and simmer for 20 to 30 minutes or until tender and two-thirds of the water has evaporated. Using a food mill fitted with the fine blade or a food processor, puree the mixture and return it to the saucepan. Beat in the butter, and season with salt and freshly ground white pepper to taste. Set the pan over another containing simmering water, cover and let cook for 20 to 30 minutes more. (The parsnip puree improves in flavor with this additional cooking.)

Nutritional Analysis *per serving: 147 calories; 19% calories from fat; 3 grams of fat; 376 milligrams of sodium*

JULIA'S MASHED POTATOES

I could hardly wait for the cooking segment the day that Julia Child came on *GMA* with her eight food processors filled with one of my favorite foods: mashed potatoes. To each food processor, she added a different and unique flavor. What a simple idea. Why didn't I think of that? I'm not Julia Child.

Serves 4 to 6 (8 to 12 if equal-portion options are used)

4 large baking potatoes (about 2½ to 2¾ pounds total), peeled and cut into quarters
Salt
Milk and/or cream to taste, heated
Soft unsalted butter, to taste
Salt and freshly ground white pepper to taste

OPTIONAL INGREDIENTS:
Equal portions of peeled, steamed, and pureed celery root, rutabaga, or snow peas, seasoned with butter and salt to taste
Equal portion of mashed baked sweet potato seasoned with grated fresh ginger and butter to taste

8 garlic cloves peeled and slowly sautéed, then mashed and mixed with a little cream

In a saucepan, combine the potatoes with lightly salted water to cover. Bring the mixture to a boil and simmer for 20 minutes or until tender. Drain the potatoes, return them to the pan, and cook them over moderate heat for 2 to 3 minutes, stirring. (This helps remove any excess moisture.) Mash the potatoes with a potato masher or food mill fitted with the fine blade. Beat in driblets of hot milk and/or cream, alternating with soft butter, and salt and freshly ground white pepper to taste. Either stir or "marble" in any optional ingredients (if using).

OUR VERSION OF JULIA'S MASHED POTATOES

Serves 6

4 large baking potatoes (about 2½ to 2¾ pounds total), peeled and quartered
Salt
1¼ to 1½ cups 2% milk, heated

¼ cup low-fat sour cream
Optional flavorings:
Equal portions of peeled, steamed, and pureed celery root, rutabaga, or snow peas, seasoned with 2 tablespoons butter and some salt
Equal portion of mashed baked sweet potato, seasoned with 2 teaspoons

grated fresh ginger, 2 tablespoons but-
ter, and some salt
8 garlic cloves, peeled, wrapped in alu-
minum foil, and roasted in a 400°F.
oven for 20 minutes or until tender,
and then mashed

In a saucepan, combine the potatoes with lightly salted water to cover. Bring the mixture to a boil and simmer for 20 minutes or until tender. Drain the potatoes, return them to the pan, and cook them over moderate heat for 2 to 3 minutes, stirring. (This helps remove any excess moisture.) Mash the potatoes with a potato masher or food mill fitted with a fine blade. Stir in the milk, sour cream, and salt and freshly ground white pepper to taste. Either stir or "marble" in any of the optional ingredients (if using).

Nutritional Analysis *per serving, without options: 202 calo-*
ries; 9 calories from fat; 2 grams of fat; 56 milligrams of
sodium

Joan and Julia

SWEET POTATO AND PARSNIP CASSEROLE

I love the way the flavors of sweet potatoes and parsnips blend together in this terrific recipe from Steven Raichlen.

Serves 4

2 cups sliced onion
2 to 3 garlic cloves, sliced, optional
2 teaspoons olive oil plus 1 teaspoon for drizzling
2 sweet potatoes (1¼ to 1½ pounds total), peeled and cut into ¼-inch slices
½ pound parsnips, peeled and cut into ¼-inch slices
1 to 1½ cups Vegetable Stock (page 204) or Chicken Broth (page 203) or canned low-sodium chicken broth
½ cup nonfat or low-fat sour cream
½ teaspoon dried thyme
Salt and pepper to taste
¼ cup fine dry bread crumbs

Preheat the oven to 400°F.

In a large skillet, cook the onions and garlic (if using) in 2 teaspoons of the oil, covered, over moderately low heat for 10 minutes or until the onions are softened. Uncover the pan, and cook the mixture for 3 minutes longer or until lightly browned. Add the potatoes, parsnips, broth, sour cream, thyme, and salt and pepper to taste, and bring the mixture to a boil. Simmer the mixture for 15 to 20 minutes or until the potatoes are tender and most of the liquid is absorbed. Taste for seasoning and add more salt and pepper if necessary.

Transfer the mixture to a shallow casserole or gratin dish in which the vegetables fit in just one layer. Sprinkle the bread crumbs evenly over the top of the casserole, and drizzle with the remaining olive oil. Bake the casserole for 20 to 30 minutes or until all the remaining broth has been absorbed and the top is crusty and brown.

Nutritional Analysis *per serving: 315 calories; 12% calories from fat; 5 grams of fat; 302 milligrams of sodium*

TWICE-BAKED PARMESAN POTATOES

A twist on the classic twice-baked potatoes, only here the fat's reduced by omitting the cheddar cheese, butter, and cream, and substituting low-fat milk, plus a small amount of pungent Parmesan cheese. Leeks add a pleasantly mild onion flavor.

Serves 4

2 baking potatoes (about 1¼ to 1½
  pounds total)
1 leek, white and pale green part only,
  finely chopped, rinsed well and patted
  dry (about ½ cup), or ½ medium
  onion, finely chopped
1 tablespoon olive oil
⅓ cup plus 2 tablespoons 1% milk,
  heated
2 tablespoons plus 2 teaspoons freshly
  grated Parmesan
Salt and pepper to taste
2 teaspoons finely chopped parsley

Preheat the oven to 425°F.

Prick the potatoes a few times with a knife, and bake them in the preheated oven for 1 hour or until tender. Let them cool until they can be handled.

While the potatoes are baking, in a nonstick skillet cook the leeks in the oil over moderately low heat for 5 minutes or until they are softened. Cut the potatoes in half lengthwise and scoop the pulp into a bowl, leaving a ¼-inch-thick shell. Mash the pulp with a fork or a potato masher until it is smooth. Stir in the cooked leeks, the milk, 2 tablespoons of the Parmesan, and salt and pepper to taste.

Mound one-quarter of the potato mixture back into the shells. Sprinkle ½ teaspoon of the remaining Parmesan over the top of each mound, and bake the stuffed potatoes in the preheated oven for 10 to 15 minutes or until they are hot. To serve, sprinkle each portion with some of the parsley.

Nutritional Analysis *per serving: 216 calories; 21% calories from fat; 5 grams of fat; 99 milligrams of sodium*

M O M ' S   R O A S T E D   N E W   P O T A T O E S

We all take different food memories from our childhood. My mom's roasted potatoes still vividly remind me of her cooking and her comforting presence in the kitchen. They're so easy to make and can be served with just about anything.

Serves 4 to 6

1½ pounds small red potatoes (about 1½
 to 2 inches in diameter), scrubbed and
 patted dry
1 tablespoon olive oil
2 tablespoons chopped fresh rosemary (or
 2 teaspoons dried)
Salt to taste

Preheat the oven to 450°F.
Cut the potatoes in half. Pour the oil into a jelly roll pan or small baking pan in which the potatoes will fit in one layer. Heat the pan in the oven for about 3 minutes or until the oil is hot, and swirl the oil to coat the bottom of the pan. Add the potatoes, cut side down, sprinkle them with the rosemary and salt to taste. Roast them for 15 to 20 minutes or until they are tender and the cut side is golden brown.

Nutritional Analysis *per serving: 120 calories; 18% calories from fat; 2 grams of fat; 5 milligrams of sodium*

ROASTED VEGETABLES

When I learned the secret of roasting vegetables, a whole new world of cooking opened up to me. Enormous flavor is added by the roasting process. Use a light brushing of olive oil to prevent vegetables from sticking to the pan. That small amount adds minimal calories and fat.

Serves 6

2 carrots, peeled and cut into sticks (about 3×½ inches)
2 parsnips, peeled and cut into sticks (about 3×½ inches)
1 zucchini, cut into sticks (about 3×½ inches)
1 red pepper, cut into strips
1 bunch asparagus (about 12 stalks), the tough ends removed and the stalk peeled
Florets from 1 head of broccoli
2 tablespoons olive oil
Salt and pepper to taste

Preheat the oven to 425°F.
Arrange all the vegetables in one layer in a large shallow roasting pan, sprinkle them with the oil, and salt and pepper to taste. Roast them, stirring once, for 10 minutes or until they are tender.

Nutritional Analysis *per serving: 139 calories; 30% calories from fat; 5 grams of fat; 41 milligrams of sodium*

GRILLED PORTOBELLO MUSHROOMS

These are an incredibly simple accompaniment to any meat you are grilling — or to add to any assortment of roasted vegetables. Portobellos have a meatier texture than button mushrooms. This is absolutely one of my favorite recipes in the book.

Serves 4

¼ *cup reduced-sodium soy sauce*
½ *teaspoon garlic powder*
1 *tablespoon olive oil*
Freshly ground black pepper to taste
4 *large portobello mushrooms, stems discarded and caps wiped clean*

Prepare the grill.
In a bowl, whisk together the soy sauce, garlic powder, olive oil, and black pepper to taste. Dip the mushrooms in the marinade, and grill them on a rack set 4 inches over the glowing coals, basting them frequently, for 5 minutes on each side or until they are tender. (Alternatively, grill the mushrooms in a ridged grill pan or broil them set on a rack 4 inches from the preheated broiler.)

Nutritional Analysis *per serving: 43 calories; 72% calories from fat; 4 grams of fat; 66 milligrams of sodium*

CORNBREAD STUFFING

Joan and Charlie

Makes about 2 quarts

FOR THE CORNBREAD:

1 cup cornmeal
½ cup all-purpose flour
1 tablespoon sugar
1 tablespoon baking powder
½ teaspoon baking soda
1 cup buttermilk
2 large eggs, lightly beaten
1 tablespoon canola oil
One 8½-ounce can cream-style corn
1 teaspoon dried sage
1 teaspoon dried rosemary or thyme
Nonstick vegetable oil spray

FOR THE STUFFING:

2 medium onions, chopped (about 2 cups)
*2 cups peeled and finely diced butternut
    squash (about ½ medium)*
*1 Golden Delicious or Granny Smith
    apple, peeled, cored, and finely diced*
2 tablespoons olive oil
1½ cups chopped celery
1 large egg, lightly beaten
½ cup apple juice
*¼ cup chicken broth (page 203) or
    canned reduced-sodium broth*
Salt and pepper to taste

Preheat the oven to 400°F.

Make the cornbread: Sift the first five ingredients into a large mixing bowl. In another bowl whisk together the buttermilk, eggs, oil, corn, and dried herbs, and stir the buttermilk mixture into the flour mixture, stirring until it is just combined. Pour the batter into an 8-inch square baking pan that has been sprayed with the nonstick vegetable oil spray and bake the cornbread in the preheated oven for 20 minutes or until a skewer, when inserted, comes out clean. Transfer the cornbread to a rack and let it cool. When it is completely cool, cut it into cubes or coarsely crumble it and transfer it to a mixing bowl.

Make the stuffing: Arrange the onion, squash, and apple in one layer in a shallow roasting pan, toss with the olive oil, and roast them in the preheated oven for 30 minutes. Add the celery and roast the vegetables for an additional 5 minutes. Transfer the vegetables to the bowl with the cornbread, along with the egg, the apple juice, the chicken broth, and salt and pepper to taste and stir gently. Transfer the mixture to a casserole dish that has been sprayed with nonstick vegetable oil spray. Cover tightly and bake for 20 minutes at 350°F. Turn up the heat to 450°F. and bake, uncovered, for 10 more minutes or until golden on top.

Optional: If you want to make the dish more hearty, add 1 pound crumbled, cooked, and drained lean turkey or chicken sausage.

QUICK CHILI BEANS

This is an unusually quick way to make chili, since most versions require hours of cooking. When time is a factor, this easy dish will complement almost any roast meat or rice dish, or can be served as a meal in itself.

Makes about 3 cups

1 medium onion, chopped (about 1 cup)
2 garlic cloves, minced (about 2 tea-
    spoons)
2 teaspoons olive oil
1 teaspoon ground cumin
1 tablespoon chili powder
2 fifteen-ounce cans pinto, kidney, or
    black beans, drained and rinsed
¾ cup Chicken Broth (page 203) or
    canned reduced-sodium chicken broth
1 tablespoon tomato paste
1 tablespoon red wine vinegar
Salt and pepper to taste

In a saucepan, cook the onion and the garlic in the oil over moderately low heat for 5 minutes, or until softened. Add the cumin and chili powder, and cook for 3 minutes. Add all the remaining ingredients, and simmer for 10 minutes. Add salt and pepper to taste.

Nutritional Analysis *per ½-cup serving: 101 calories; 20% calories from fat; 3 grams of fat; 374 milligrams of sodium*

Chapter 14

SAUCES, SALSAS, BROTHS, STOCKS, AND MARINADES

ROASTED FRESH TOMATO SAUCE

Roasting the tomatoes in the oven before making this homemade sauce brings out a wonderful depth of flavor. Freeze and use in place of canned sauce.

Makes about 5 cups

4 pounds ripe, unblemished plum tomatoes
1 medium onion, coarsely chopped (about 1 cup)
8 to 10 garlic cloves, or to taste, peeled
2 tablespoons extra-virgin olive oil
Salt and pepper to taste
Optional flavoring:
2 tablespoons chopped fresh herbs (such as basil, rosemary, dill, oregano, chives, or parsley)

Preheat the oven to 400°F.
Cut the tomatoes lengthwise into quarters, and arrange them in one layer in a shallow roasting pan. Sprinkle the onion and the garlic around the tomatoes, and drizzle the oil over the vegetables. Roast the vegetables for 50 to 60 minutes or until the tomatoes are lightly browned and the garlic is tender when pierced with a knife. Transfer the mixture, in batches, to a food processor, and chop coarsely or puree until fine (to produce either a chunky or a smooth sauce). Add salt and pepper to taste, and the chopped herbs (if using).

Nutritional Analysis *per ½-cup serving: 72 calories; 37% calories from fat; 3 grams of fat; 17 milligrams of sodium*

WINTER TOMATO SAUCE

You can have fresh tomato sauce even in the dead of winter — if you use canned plum tomatoes, which are far better then than the fresh. A bit of tomato paste provides the extra oomph.

Makes about 3½ cups

1 medium onion, chopped (about 1 cup)
1 tablespoon extra-virgin olive oil
3 garlic cloves, minced (about 1 heaping tablespoon)
35-ounce can Italian plum tomatoes, chopped, juice reserved
2 tablespoons tomato paste
Salt and pepper to taste
Optional flavorings:
1 teaspoon dried oregano, basil, or rosemary

In a large nonstick skillet, cook the onion in the oil over moderately low heat for 5 minutes, or until it is softened. Add the garlic and cook for 5 minutes, or until the mixture is just golden. Add the tomatoes with their juice, the tomato paste, and the herbs (if using). Bring to a boil and simmer for 20 minutes or until thickened. Add salt and pepper to taste.

Nutritional Analysis *per ½-cup serving: 60 calories; 32% calories from fat; 2 grams of fat; 269 milligrams of sodium*

CRANBERRY-STRAWBERRY-PINEAPPLE RELISH

I call this recipe "the gift that keeps on giving." Grandma Joie gave it to me, and I've passed it along to so many people I've lost count. Although it's a real winner on the Thanksgiving table with turkey, don't tuck it away to be used only once a year. I've used it with a lot of other dishes, such as chicken or pork.

Makes about 6½ cups

2 sixteen-ounce cans whole-berry cran-
    berry sauce
20-ounce can crushed pineapple, drained
20-ounce bag defrosted frozen strawber-
    ries, drained and coarsely chopped

OPTIONAL ADDITIONS:
12-ounce bag defrosted frozen raspber-
    ries, drained
½ cup chopped toasted walnuts

In a large bowl, combine all the ingredients (with the optional additions, if using) and chill well.

Nutritional Analysis *per ¼-cup serving: 86 calories; 0% calories from fat; 0 grams of fat; 10 milligrams of sodium*

RAITA

This cucumber-yogurt sauce, with its fresh, tangy taste, comes from my favorite Indian restaurant: the Bengal Tiger in White Plains, New York. Its simple flavor is light and tasty. It works especially well as a dip for chips, or an accompaniment for chicken or lamb.

Makes about 2 cups

1½ cups peeled, seeded, and coarsely
    shredded cucumber (about ¾ pound)
1½ cups plain nonfat yogurt
½ teaspoon salt
1 tablespoon finely chopped fresh mint
    (or 1 teaspoon dried)
½ teaspoon paprika

In a bowl, stir together the cucumber, the yogurt, and the salt. Transfer the mixture to a serving bowl, and sprinkle with the mint and the paprika.

Nutritional Analysis *per ¼-cup serving: 27 calories; 4% calories from fat; Trace amount of fat; 166 milligrams of sodium*

MANGO OR PAPAYA SALSA

Papaya is one of my favorite fruits. I use this easy and delicious salsa to accompany fish, poultry, and meat. You can use mango as a substitute for papaya, or even split the flavors fifty-fifty.

Makes about 2 cups

1 firm-ripe medium mango or papaya, peeled, seeded, and finely diced (about 2 cups)
½ small red onion, chopped fine (about ¼ cup), soaked in cold water for 20 minutes and drained
1 jalapeño, minced, or ½ teaspoon hot sauce
3 tablespoons fresh lime juice
2 tablespoons chopped fresh coriander or basil
½ teaspoon salt, optional, or to taste

In a bowl, combine well all the ingredients, add salt to taste (if using), and chill for at least 30 minutes before serving.

Nutritional Analysis *per 2-tablespoon serving: 11 calories; 3% calories from fat; Trace amount of fat; 0 milligrams of sodium*

CHICKEN BROTH

I like to make chicken broth and keep it in the freezer. I use it as a substitute for oil in pasta recipes, or as a flavor enhancer for chicken dishes. Try experimenting on your own. You will be surprised at how often you use this delicious secret weapon in your low-fat diet.

Makes about 10 cups

5 pounds chicken wings, rinsed
4 quarts water
1 medium onion, coarsely chopped (about
  1 cup)
1 carrot, coarsely chopped
1 celery stalk, coarsely chopped
1 bay leaf
1 teaspoon dried thyme
3 parsley sprigs

In a large kettle, combine the chicken wings with the water and bring the mixture to a boil, skimming the scum that rises to the surface. Simmer the stock for 20 minutes, skimming as needed, and add the remaining ingredients. Bring the stock back to a boil, and simmer for 1 hour and 40 minutes, adding additional water if necessary. Strain the stock and skim off the fat.

Nutritional Analysis *per 1-cup serving: 22 calories; 43% calories from fat; 1 gram of fat; 172 milligrams of sodium*

VEGETABLE STOCK

Vegetable stock is an ideal solution for those who want a homemade vegetarian broth — one with far less sodium than canned.

Makes about 10 cups

2 medium onions, cut into eighths
2 small leeks (white and green part),
    chopped coarse and rinsed well
2 carrots, cut into 2-inch lengths
2 parsnips, cut into 2-inch lengths
1 cup chopped tomato (fresh or canned)
6 garlic cloves, peeled
4 parsley sprigs
1 bay leaf
½ teaspoon dried thyme
4 quarts water

In a large kettle, combine all the ingredients and bring to a boil. Simmer for 1½ hours and strain.

Nutritional Analysis *per 1-cup serving: 27 calories; 5% calories from fat; Trace amount of fat; 19 milligrams of sodium*

MARINADE FOR EVERYTHING BUT WAFFLES AND HOT DOGS

The name says it all. Use on anything, everything . . . okay, almost everything.

Makes 3 cups

2 cups Dijon mustard
9 garlic cloves, crushed (3 tablespoons)
1 tablespoon lemon pepper
2 teaspoons fines herbes seasoning (or a combination of parsley, chervil, chives, and tarragon)
½ cup white or red wine vinegar (or a mixture of half fresh lemon juice and half vinegar)
½ cup Reduced-Fat Italian Dressing (page 124) or your favorite purchased low-fat or nonfat brand
⅓ cup reduced-sodium soy sauce
Optional flavorings:
2 tablespoons Liquid Smoke
3 to 4 shakes hot sauce
Red pepper flakes to taste

In a bowl, whisk together the mustard, garlic, lemon pepper, and fines herbes. Add the vinegar, Italian dressing, soy sauce, and any optional flavorings (if using).

Nutritional Analysis *per tablespoon: 31 calories; 65% calories from fat; 2 grams of fat; 493 milligrams of sodium*

Chapter 15

❖

FUN RECIPES FOR YOUR KIDS
GRILLED CHEESE PITA
SANDWICHES

These quick lunchtime sandwiches combine two favorites — pocket bread sandwiches and grilled cheese — to make a new favorite.

Serves 4

4 six-inch plain or whole-wheat pitas
4 ounces low-fat cheese (cheddar, moz-
*   zarella, or Swiss), shredded or coarsely*
*   grated*
Nonstick vegetable oil spray
Optional additions (per sandwich):
2 thin slices tomato
3 thin slices onion
1 piece crumbled, cooked turkey bacon
4 thin rounds dill pickle
1 small mushroom, sliced
1 tablespoon sliced, pitted olives

Cut a small slice from one side of each pita to make an opening, and stuff one-fourth of the cheese and any optional additions into each opening. (Make sure that any optional addition is wedged in the middle of the cheese, so that the cheese melts evenly and the pita stays crisp.)

In a preheated large skillet that has been sprayed with the nonstick vegetable spray, cook the stuffed pitas over moderate heat, covered, for 5 minutes a side or until crispy on both sides.

Nutritional Analysis *per serving, with all optional additions: 262 calories; 32% calories from fat; 9 grams of fat; 841 milligrams of sodium*

Nutritional Analysis *per serving, without any optional additions: 185 calories; 23% calories from fat; 5 grams of fat; 355 milligrams of sodium*

❖

EASY MACARONI AND CHEESE

Who doesn't love macaroni and cheese — and where would American moms be without it? Treat the family to a homemade version that cuts out much of the usual fat by using skim milk and reduced-fat or low-fat cheddar.

Serves 4 to 6

1½ tablespoons unsalted butter
2 tablespoons all-purpose flour
1½ cups skim milk, heated
8 ounces low-fat cheddar cheese (2 cups),
*   coarsely grated*
1 box (7 to 8 ounces) dried macaroni
Salt and pepper to taste

In a saucepan, melt the butter over low heat. Whisk in the flour and cook the mixture, stirring, for 3 minutes. Add the milk, in a stream, whisking. Bring the mixture to a boil, and simmer for 3 minutes. Stir in the cheese and cook until all the cheese is melted.

Cook the macaroni according to package instructions, and drain well.

Combine with cheese mixture and salt and pepper to taste.

Nutritional Analysis *per serving: 294 calories; 31% calories from fat; 10 grams of fat; 314 milligrams of sodium*

PITA PIZZA

This is a great dinner for the kids, especially if you put assorted toppings in dishes on the counter and let them build their own. It's fun, it's healthy, and it's nutritious, too.

Makes 4 pizzas

2 six- or seven-inch pitas, each one split into 2 rounds
½ cup Roasted Fresh Tomato Sauce (page 197) or your favorite purchased brand
1 cup coarsely grated low-fat or part-skim mozzarella

OPTIONAL TOPPINGS *(per pizza):*
2 sliced mushrooms
1 tablespoon sliced black olives
1 tablespoon chopped red or green bell pepper
¼ cup sliced onion
1 tablespoon sliced sun-dried tomatoes (not oil-packed), rehydrated*
2 tablespoons shredded fresh basil leaves

Preheat the oven to 425°F.

Arrange pita rounds cut side up on a baking sheet. Spread 2 tablespoons of the tomato sauce evenly on top of each one, and sprinkle 4 tablespoons of the mozzarella over the tomato sauce. Add any of the optional toppings, and bake the pizzas in the oven for 8 to 10 minutes, or until the cheese is melted.

*To rehydrate sun-dried tomatoes: Pour boiling water to cover over the tomatoes, and let them stand for 20 minutes. Drain and pat dry.

Nutritional Analysis *per pizza, with all optional toppings: 164 calories; 22% calories from fat; 4 grams of fat; 425 milligrams of sodium*

Nutritional Analysis *per pizza, without any optional toppings: 122 calories; 17% calories from fat; 2 grams of fat; 363 milligrams of sodium*

S A R A H ' S   L A S A G N A

Sarah Krauss

So easy, even a kid can do it. And one does. My nine-year-old, Sarah, says she's really proud when she makes our family dinner all by herself. This is easy, quick, healthy — and everyone in the family loves it.

Serves 6 to 8

3 cups Roasted Fresh Tomato Sauce (page 197) or your favorite purchased brand
12 dried lasagna noodles, cooked according to package directions and drained
8 ounces nonfat or part-skim mozzarella cheese, coarsely grated
2 cups nonfat or part-skim ricotta cheese
½ cup freshly grated Parmesan cheese

Preheat the oven to 350°F.

In the bottom of a 13×9-inch baking dish, spread about ¼ cup of the tomato sauce. Arrange four of the lasagna noodles on top of the sauce in one layer, overlapping them slightly. Spread one-third of the remaining tomato sauce on top of the noodles, one-third of the mozzarella on top of the sauce, one-half of the ricotta on top of the mozzarella and one-third of the Parmesan on top of the ricotta. Repeat the procedure for the next layer. For the last layer, spread the remaining sauce on top of the noodles, the remaining mozzarella on top of the sauce, and the remaining Parmesan on top of the mozzarella.

Bake the lasagna in the preheated oven for 40 minutes, or until it is bubbly and heated through.

Nutritional Analysis *per serving: 311 calories; 15% calories from fat; 5 grams of fat; 435 milligrams of sodium*

LINDSAY'S TASTY TACOS

Lindsay Krauss

Tacos are on the exclusive list of Six Things My Kids Will Eat in Life. The trick is how to vary those items and keep your kids happy. Put out bowls of optional toppings and let the kids be creative. When kids choose their own foods, they're more likely to eat.

Makes 12 tacos

1 medium onion, chopped (about 1 cup)
2 garlic cloves, minced (about 2 tea-
　spoons)
2 tablespoons vegetable oil
1 pound ground raw turkey
1 tablespoon chili powder
1 cup Roasted Fresh Tomato Sauce (page
　197) or your favorite purchased brand
1 cup Chicken Broth (page 203) or
　canned reduced-sodium chicken broth
Salt and pepper to taste
12 taco shells

GARNISHES:
1 cup shredded iceberg lettuce
1 cup coarsely grated carrots
1 cup shredded low-fat Monterey Jack or
　cheddar cheese
1 cup nonfat plain yogurt, or low-fat
　sour cream
½ cup sliced, pitted olives, optional

Preheat the oven to 350°F.

In a large nonstick skillet, cook the onion and the garlic in the oil over moderately low heat for 5 minutes or until the onion is softened. Add the turkey, and cook the mixture over moderate heat for 5 minutes or until the turkey is no longer pink. Add the chili powder, and cook for 2 minutes. Add the tomato sauce and the chicken broth, and simmer for 15 minutes. Add salt and pepper to taste.

Meanwhile, arrange the taco shells on a baking sheet and heat them in the preheated oven for 5 to 7 minutes or until warm.

To serve, spoon the turkey mixture into the shells and top with the garnishes.

Nutritional Analysis *per taco, with all optional toppings: 183 calories; 49% calories from fat; 10 grams of fat; 304 milligrams of sodium*

Nutritional Analysis *per taco, without any optional toppings: 132 calories; 50% calories from fat; 8 grams of fat; 205 milligrams of sodium*

UNFRIED CHICKEN

In a million years, I never thought there would be a way to cook fried chicken that wasn't fattening. So when I first heard about this oven "frying" method, I was sure someone was pulling my leg . . . or should that be "drumstick"? Anyway, having tried it, I can say it's definitely worth crowing about.

Serves 4

¼ cup white or whole wheat flour
¼ cup crushed cornflakes or cornmeal
½ teaspoon Italian seasoning or oregano
Salt and pepper to taste
3½-pound chicken, cut into 8 pieces* (reserving the chicken wings for another use such as Chicken Broth — page 203) and the skin discarded
2 egg whites, beaten lightly

Preheat the oven to 350°F.

In a shallow bowl, toss together the flour, cornflakes, Italian seasoning, and salt and pepper to taste. Dip the chicken pieces in the egg whites, and then coat them all over with the flour mixture. Arrange the chicken in one layer on a rack in a shallow roasting pan, and bake it in the oven for 1 hour.

Note: Other spices could be added to the flour mixture, such as ½ teaspoon thyme, rosemary, or paprika, or ¼ teaspoon cayenne.

*2 thigh pieces, 2 leg pieces, 2 breast pieces cut into 2 pieces.

Nutritional Analysis *per serving: 331 calories; 28% calories from fat; 10 grams of fat; 172 milligrams of sodium*

GRANDMA JOIE'S POTATO PANCAKES

My kids love potato pancakes. Okay, all right, so do I — especially accompanied by applesauce and sour cream. Just choose a reduced-fat or nonfat sour cream and enjoy!

Serves 4 to 6

1 small onion, peeled and quartered
2 baking potatoes (about 1¼ to 1½
  pounds total), peeled and cut length-
  wise into quarters
¼ teaspoon salt, optional
Freshly ground black pepper
Nonstick vegetable oil spray
Applesauce and low-fat or nonfat sour
  cream for garnish, optional

Using a food processor fitted with the grating blade, grate the onion and then the potato. (Alternatively, coarsely grate the onion and the potato with a hand-held four-sided grater.)

Transfer the mixture to a bowl, and add the salt and freshly ground black pepper to taste.

Spray an 8-inch nonstick skillet with the nonstick vegetable oil spray, and heat it over moderately high heat. Add the potato mixture and pat it down firmly to form a 7-inch round about ½ inch thick. Turn down the heat to moderate, and cook the pancake about 10 to 15 minutes a side or until it is golden.

(Hint: to turn the potato over easily, slide it onto a pot lid that is slightly larger than the pancake, and then invert it back into the pan.)

Cut the potato pancake into wedges, and serve it with the applesauce and sour cream (if using).

Nutritional Analysis *per serving, without applesauce or sour cream: 110 calories; 1% calories from fat; trace amount of fat; 6 milligrams of sodium*

Chapter 16

❖

DESSERTS

ANGEL FOOD CAKE WITH
CHOCOLATE SAUCE

This angel food cake recipe comes from cookbook author Ruth Spears. You can serve it with either a chocolate or a raspberry sauce. If you are really daring, try serving with both!

Serves 12

1 cup sifted cake flour
1½ cups sifted superfine sugar
1½ cups egg whites (about 12 large), at
    room temperature
1 teaspoon cream of tartar
½ teaspoon salt
1 teaspoon vanilla extract
½ teaspoon almond extract
1 teaspoon fresh lemon juice
Low-Fat Chocolate Sauce or Raspberry
    Sauce (recipes follow), as an accompa-
    niment

Preheat the oven to 325°F.

Sift the flour 6 times with ½ cup of the already-sifted sugar and set the mixture aside.

In a very large bowl, combine the egg whites with the cream of tartar and the salt, and beat the mixture with an electric mixer just until stiff peaks form. Sift a little of the remaining cup of sugar over the whites, and gently fold in with a whisk. Repeat gradually until all the sugar is incorporated. Then sift a little of the reserved sugar/flour mixture over the egg whites, and fold it in. Repeat gradually until it

is all incorporated. Fold in the vanilla and almond extracts and the lemon juice.

Turn the batter into an ungreased 10-inch tube pan. Bake about 1 hour, then test by pressing lightly in the center. If the cake springs back, it is done. If not, bake up to 15 minutes more, testing at 5-minute intervals.

Remove the pan from the oven, invert it on a rack, and let the cake cool for 1½ hours. The pan must be raised from the countertop at least 1 inch or so while this takes place. When thoroughly cooled, remove the cake from the pan by loosening the sides with a metal spatula.

To serve, pierce with a fork at intervals to mark portions, and pull apart with two forks to avoid mashing the cake. Serve with either the chocolate sauce, the raspberry sauce, or a little bit of both sauces.

Nutritional Analysis *per serving, without Low-Fat Chocolate Sauce or Raspberry Sauce: 143 calories; 0% calories from fat; 0 grams of fat; 144 milligrams of sodium*

LOW-FAT CHOCOLATE SAUCE

Makes 1¼ cups

2 ounces bittersweet chocolate, coarsely
    chopped
1 tablespoon instant espresso, dissolved in
    2 tablespoons boiling water
½ cup evaporated skim milk
3 tablespoons unsweetened cocoa
⅓ cup sugar
2 teaspoons cornstarch
3 tablespoons light corn syrup
2 tablespoons Kahlúa

In a bowl, combine the chocolate with the espresso powder and water. Bring the milk just to a boil over medium heat, and pour over the chocolate mixture, stirring until all of the chocolate is melted.

In a saucepan, stir together the cocoa, sugar, and cornstarch. Add the milk mixture and the corn syrup, stirring well to combine.

Bring the sauce to a boil over medium heat, and boil for 1 minute or until thickened. Remove from heat and stir in Kahlúa. Cool completely and refrigerate until serving.

Nutritional Analysis *per 1-tablespoon serving: 46 calories; 30% calories from fat; 2 grams of fat; 10 milligrams of sodium*

RASPBERRY SAUCE

Makes about ¾ cup

One 12-ounce bag frozen raspberries,
    defrosted
¼ cup confectioner's sugar
2 teaspoons fresh lemon juice

In a food processor, puree the raspberries. Strain the mixture through a sieve and discard the seeds. Stir in the confectioner's sugar and the lemon juice.

Nutritional Analysis *per 2-tablespoon serving: 44 calories; 6% calories from fat; trace amount of fat; 0 milligrams of sodium*

PEACH MELBA WITH RASPBERRY SAUCE

Inspired by my favorite dessert from the Mirror Lake Inn in Lake Placid, New York, this combination of flavors is unparalleled. The original Melba recipe was created in the late 1800s by famed French chef Escoffier for Dame Nellie Melba, a popular Australian opera singer. It's still a dessert to please any diva.

Serves 6

6 ripe peaches
Raspberry Sauce (page 216)
¾ pint frozen vanilla yogurt
Mint sprigs for garnish

Halve the peaches by cutting along the natural indentation and then twisting to separate. Remove the pit with a spoon. Spoon 2 tablespoons of the sauce on each of six chilled plates. Arrange two peach halves cut side up on top of the sauce, and scoop ⅛ cup of the frozen yogurt into the cavity of each peach half. Garnish with mint sprigs.

Nutritional Analysis *per serving: 141 calories; 5% calories from fat; 1 gram of fat; 3 milligrams of sodium*

VANILLA CHEESECAKE WITH FRESH BERRIES

Healthy cheesecake? It's true — with only 21 percent of the calories from fat, thanks to a luscious combination of cream cheese, sour cream (both reduced-fat), vanilla yogurt, and cottage cheese. Fresh berries top it all off.

Serves 8 to 10

4 cups (32 ounces) low-fat vanilla yogurt
Nonstick vegetable oil spray
¾ cup chocolate wafer crumbs (3 ounces or about 12 to 13 cookies)
2 cups 1% cottage cheese, squeezed in a kitchen towel to remove any excess liquid
8 ounces low-fat cream cheese
4 ounces low-fat sour cream
1¼ cups sugar
1 large egg
2 large egg whites
1 tablespoon vanilla extract
¼ teaspoon salt
¼ cup all-purpose flour
1 pint strawberries, 1 pint blueberries, or other berries for garnish

Spoon the yogurt into a strainer lined with a wet paper towel and set over a bowl. Cover the yogurt with plastic wrap and let it drain, refrigerated, overnight. Discard the liquid that has accumulated in the bowl, and reserve the yogurt.

Preheat the oven to 325°F.

Spray the bottom and sides of a 9-inch springform pan thoroughly with the nonstick vegetable oil spray. Press the crumbs evenly into the bottom and up the sides of the pan, and set aside.

In a food processor, puree the cottage cheese until completely smooth. Add the yogurt, cream cheese, and sour cream, and process until smooth. Add the remaining ingredients except the berries, and process until well combined.

Pour the batter into the prepared springform pan, and tap the pan gently on the counter to remove any air bubbles. Bake the cheesecake in the preheated oven for 50 to 60 minutes, or until set but still slightly wobbly in the center.

Turn off the oven and leave the cheesecake in it for 30 minutes. Set the pan on a rack and let it cool completely. Chill the cheesecake at least 2 hours or overnight. Garnish with fresh berries before serving.

Nutritional Analysis *per serving: 346 calories; 21% calories from fat; 8 grams of fat; 524 milligrams of sodium*

COUNTRY APPLE PIE

Group entertaining shot

What would a family cookbook be without good old-fashioned apple pie? This rustic variation combines Patsy Jamieson's recipe for the crust with a healthy, delicious filling created by my recipe chef, Sara Moulton. This French-style tart is far easier to make than the traditional pie. The dough is simply rolled out into a circle, and the apples are placed on top. Serve the dessert warm with your favorite low-fat frozen vanilla yogurt. The whole treat still comes in with less than 30 percent of calories from fat.

Serves 10

FOR THE CRUST:

2 tablespoons unsalted butter
3 tablespoons plus 1 teaspoon canola oil
1½ cups all-purpose flour
2 tablespoons sugar
½ teaspoon salt
3 to 6 tablespoons ice water
Nonstick vegetable spray

FOR THE PIE FILLING:

5 to 6 Golden Delicious apples
2½ tablespoons fresh lemon juice
¼ cup plus 3 tablespoons sugar
½ teaspoon cinnamon
¼ cup apricot preserves
Low-fat frozen vanilla yogurt as an accompaniment, optional

Preheat the oven to 425° F.

Set the oven rack in the center of the oven.

In a small saucepan, melt the butter over moderate heat until it turns golden brown and emits a nutty aroma. Remove from heat, stir in canola oil, and let cool.

In a large bowl, whisk together the flour, sugar, and salt until well combined. When the butter mixture is cool, use a fork to slowly stir it into the flour mixture, until the mixture resembles coarse meal. Stir in the ice water, starting with 3 tablespoons and adding more if necessary, a teaspoon at a time, or until the dough holds together in a ball.

Roll the dough into a 14-inch circle between sheets of plastic wrap or wax paper. Remove the top sheet of wrap, and invert the dough onto a 12×17-inch baking sheet sprayed with the nonstick vegetable oil spray. Cover the dough and chill it while you prepare the apples.

Peel and core the apples and cut into eighths. Toss with the lemon juice, ¼ cup of the sugar, and the cinnamon. On top of the rolled-out pie dough, arrange the apple slices, slightly overlapping in concentric circles. Fold the pastry border over the apples to form an edge and sprinkle them with the remaining 3 tablespoons of sugar.

Bake the pie for 15 minutes, reduce the heat to 375°F., and bake for 30 to 40 minutes more or until the crust is golden. With a long metal spatula, loosen the bottom and slide the tart onto a platter. In a small saucepan, heat the apricot jam with 1 tablespoon of water and brush the mixture on top of the apples.

Nutritional Analysis *per serving: 233 calories; 27% calories from fat; 7 grams of fat; 108 milligrams of sodium*

CHOCOLATE PUDDING

I grew up on chocolate pudding. It was one of the desserts served most often in my house, and my daughters love it likewise. This one's for them, and for the kid in all of us who still gets that craving every now and then for a rich, smooth, creamy pudding.

Makes 6 servings

2 tablespoons sugar
¼ cup cocoa
3 tablespoons cornstarch
Pinch of salt
1½ cups evaporated skim milk
½ cup skim milk
¼ cup light or dark corn syrup
1 large egg
1 ounce bittersweet (or semisweet) chocolate, chopped

In a saucepan, whisk together the sugar, cocoa, cornstarch, and salt. Whisk in the milks and the corn syrup, and bring the mixture to a boil over moderately high heat, whisking constantly. Boil the mixture for 1 minute and remove it from the heat.

In a bowl, beat the egg lightly and whisk in 2 tablespoons of the hot chocolate mixture. Add the egg mixture to the saucepan, and cook the pudding over moderate heat for 1 minute, whisking. Stir in the bittersweet chocolate, and transfer the pudding to a bowl. Cover the surface directly with plastic wrap. Let it cool and chill well before serving.

Nutritional Analysis *per ½-cup serving: 174 calories; 14% calories from fat; 3 grams of fat; 144 milligrams of sodium*

B E R R Y   G R A T I N

Mmmmm . . . a legal scoop of warm heaven for the berry lovers in the bunch.

Makes 4 servings

2½ cups blueberries, picked over and
   stems removed
1½ cups raspberries plus 8 extra for
   garnish
1 cup blackberries
1 teaspoon cinnamon
1½ tablespoons granulated sugar
1 cup low-fat plain yogurt
1½ tablespoons honey
¼ cup firmly packed brown sugar

Preheat broiler.

In a large bowl, gently toss together the berries, cinnamon, and granulated sugar. In a small bowl, whisk together the yogurt and honey.

Divide the berry mixture among 4 individual gratin or ovenproof dishes. Top each one with ¼ cup of the yogurt mixture, and sprinkle with 1 tablespoon of the brown sugar.

Broil until the sugar melts and caramelizes, about 2 minutes. Garnish with raspberries and serve immediately.

Note: The berries can also be cooked in one large gratin pan or shallow baking dish.

Nutritional Analysis *per serving: 222 calories; 6% calories from fat; 2 grams of fat; 50 milligrams of sodium*

INDIVIDUAL STRAWBERRY OR PLUM SHORTCAKES

A dessert that's less fattening than the usual shortcakes with whipped cream. Substitute your favorite fruit at the peak of its season in the filling for variety.

Makes 8 servings

FOR THE BISCUITS:
2 cups all-purpose flour
2 teaspoons baking powder
½ teaspoon baking soda
Pinch of salt
7 tablespoons firmly packed brown sugar
4 tablespoons cold unsalted butter, cut into bits
½ cup plus 1 tablespoon buttermilk
2 tablespoons skim milk
1 tablespoon granulated sugar

1 recipe Macerated Strawberries (recipe follows), or1 recipe Vanilla Poached Plums (recipe follows)
1½ cups low-fat vanilla yogurt

Preheat the oven to 425°F.

Make the biscuits: In a large bowl, whisk together the first five ingredients. With a pastry blender or two forks, blend in the butter until the mixture resembles coarse meal. With a fork, stir in the buttermilk until the mixture forms a dough. Knead the dough six to eight times on a floured board and drop it in 8 mounds onto a buttered baking sheet. Brush the tops with skim milk, sprinkle with sugar, and bake for 15 to 20 minutes, or until golden.

Transfer to a rack to cool. If not serving immediately, cool completely and wrap tightly in plastic wrap. (Biscuits can be made up to 8 hours ahead and warmed in a 300°F. oven before serving.)

To serve: Split the biscuits around the middle with a sharp knife. Place bottoms in the center of eight dessert plates. Top each one with one-eighth of the macerated strawberries or poached plums, and 2 to 3 tablespoons of vanilla yogurt. Position the biscuit top over the yogurt.

Nutritional Analysis *per strawberry shortcake: 315 calories; 20% calories from fat; 7 grams of fat; 212 milligrams of sodium*

Nutritional Analysis *per plum shortcake: 315 calories; 20% calories from fat; 7 grams of fat; 212 milligrams of sodium*

MACERATED STRAWBERRIES

2 pints strawberries, rinsed, hulled, and
   sliced
¾ teaspoon vanilla extract
⅓ cup granulated sugar

Stir together the strawberries, vanilla, and sugar, and let stand for 30 minutes before serving.

Nutritional Analysis *per serving: 53 calories; 4% calories from fat; trace amount of fat; 1 milligram of sodium*

❖

VANILLA POACHED PLUMS

¾ cup granulated sugar
1¾ cups water
1 vanilla bean, split
8 plums, pitted and sliced

In a small saucepan, combine the sugar, water, and vanilla bean. Bring the mixture to a boil, covered, and add half the plums. Bring the mixture back to a boil. Simmer for 5 minutes, covered, and remove the plums with a slotted spoon to a bowl. Repeat the procedure with the remaining plums and chill them, covered, until they are cold. (Discard the poaching syrup.)

Nutritional Analysis *per serving: 53 calories; 6% calories from fat; Trace amount of fat; 0 milligrams of sodium*

❖

CHOCOLATE MERINGUE COOKIES

These melt-in-your-mouth cookies are a terrific almost-no-fat treat to satisfy a chocoholic's craving for a quick hit.

Makes 2 to 3 dozen

3 ounces (½ cup) semisweet chocolate morsels
2 large egg whites, at room temperature
Pinch of salt
¼ teaspoon cream of tartar
½ cup plus 2 tablespoons granulated sugar
3 tablespoons unsweetened cocoa powder

Preheat oven to 325°F.

In a metal bowl set over a pot of barely simmering water, melt the chocolate, stirring frequently. Remove from heat and cool chocolate to room temperature.

With an electric mixer, beat egg whites and salt until frothy. Add cream of tartar, and whip to soft peaks. Continue beating, adding the sugar gradually, until the mixture just forms stiff peaks when the beaters are lifted from the bowl. Fold in the cocoa and melted chocolate. Drop batter by rounded teaspoonfuls onto a foil-covered baking sheet. Bake meringues for 13 to 15 minutes until the tops have cracked and the centers are fairly dry. Cool on baking sheet for 10 minutes. Using a metal spatula, carefully transfer meringues to a rack to finish cooling.

You can store these in an airtight container for 2 days, or freeze for up to 6 months between sheets of wax paper in an airtight container.

Nutritional Analysis *per cookie: 27 calories; 23% calories from fat; 1 gram of fat; 9 milligrams of sodium*

PHOTO CREDITS

INDEX

❖